1000 European History Facts and 50 True Tales

A Journey Through Europe's Defining Moments and Figures

Welcome Aboard, Check Out This Limited-Time Free Bonus!

Ahoy, reader! Welcome to the Ahoy Publications family, and thanks for snagging a copy of this book! Since you've chosen to join us on this journey, we'd like to offer you something special.

Check out the link below for a FREE e-book filled with delightful facts about American History.

But that's not all - you'll also have access to our exclusive email list with even more free e-books and insider knowledge. Well, what are ye waiting for? Click the link below to join and set sail toward exciting adventures in American History.

Access your bonus here: https://ahoypublications.com/

Or, Scan the QR code!

Table of Contents

Part 1: European History

1000 Interesting Facts About Europe

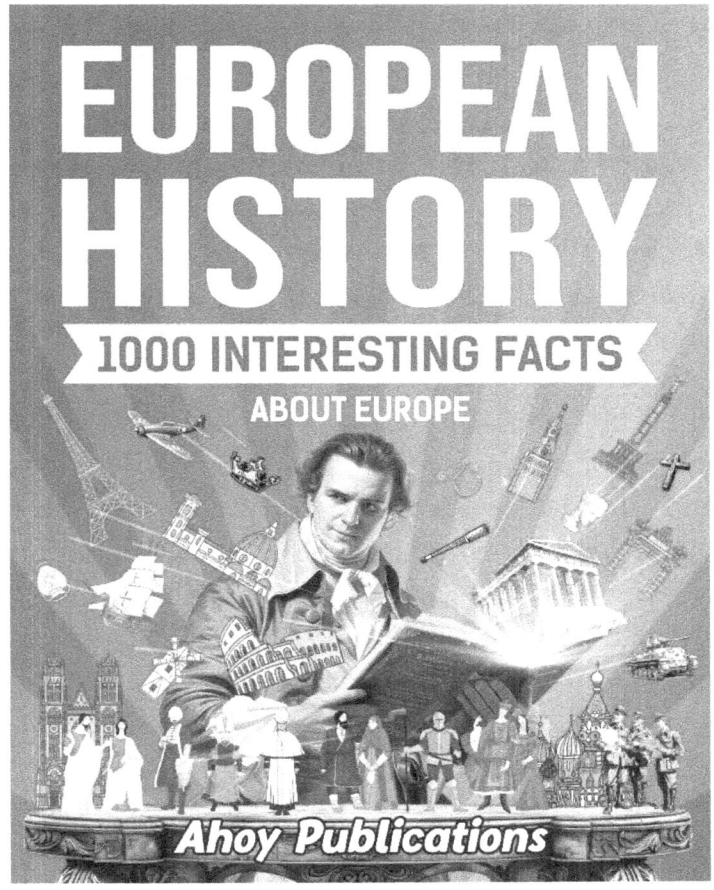

Introduction

The history of Europe is full of incredible stories and complex developments. Each period has uniquely shaped the European continent, from the Upper Paleolithic period to the fall of the Berlin Wall. **This book provides insights into this vast and varied history by exploring dozens of key events that have affected Europe.**

We begin with a look at life in **western Eurasia during the Upper Paleolithic period,** some forty thousand years ago. **Explore how human society developed over thousands of years** and how agricultural practices were first introduced during the Neolithic Revolution.

Next, we take a closer look at **ancient Greece's impressive Minoan civilization,** which was later followed by **the Mycenaean civilization.** Explore interesting facts about **the Roman Republic and the Greco-Persian War.** Discover more information about **Charlemagne's coronation** in 800 CE and **the Viking invasions** that kicked off in 790.

Gain insight into how modern-day Europe was shaped through crucial revolutions and conflicts like **the French Revolution** and **the Napoleonic Wars.**

The book concludes by exploring some of the most significant European events during modern history, including World War I and II, the Cold War, and the Greek War of Independence, just to name a few.

Get ready to journey back through time and discover the incredible **history of Europe!**

Upper Paleolithic Period
(40,000—8000 BCE)

Unravel the secrets of the last part of the Stone Age with this section. Learn twenty intriguing **facts about how people lived during this period**. Did they use fire? Did they believe in gods? Did they leave any kind of records? Let's discover the answers to these questions!

1. **The Upper Paleolithic period was the last part of the Stone Age.** It began about forty thousand years ago in Europe.

2. **During this period, people lived in hunter-gatherer societies and made tools from stone,** which they used to hunt animals like mammoths, bison, and deer.

3. **People began using fire during this period to cook food,** keep warm in cold climates, and have a form of light at night.

4. **People started creating art by painting on cave walls** and carving sculptures out of bone or ivory.

5. **Over six hundred wall paintings adorn Lascaux, a cave complex in France.** It is debated how old these paintings are, but most archaeologists agree they are around seventeen thousand years old.

6. **Archaeologists have discovered several village sites across Europe** dating back to between 18,500 and 8000 BCE.

7. In parts of **Europe, such as France and Spain, there was a culture called the Solutrean,** which lasted from around 22,000 to 17,500 BCE.

8. **The technology used by the Solutrean included spears** with sharpened points made from bones that could be thrown over long distances.

9. **The name comes from the Solutré region of France,** where the earliest remains of weapon heads of that technology were found.

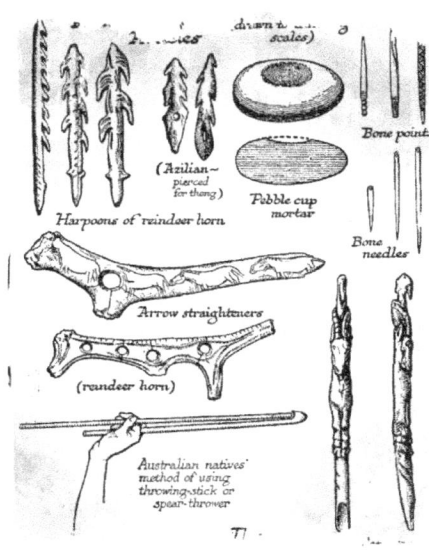

10. Another group known as **the Gravettians flourished in central Europe between 28,000 and 22,000 BCE.** These people were hunters who used horses to hunt wild animals, such as reindeer.

11. **The Gravettian culture is well known for its tools,** such as the Gravette points, which were used to hunt large animals.

12. **In some parts of Europe, people began burying their dead in tombs or graves** with offerings like jewelry and food. This was a sign they had developed spiritual beliefs.

13. **People began trading with other cultures during this period.**

14. **There was an increase in population size as people traveled farther away from their homes** in search of new resources.

15. **Clothing worn during the Upper Paleolithic included fur and leather garments.** People also wore jewelry made from animal bones or shells.

16. **Pottery would not become popular until much later.** At this time, most humans prepared food on open flames.

17. **While there is evidence that humans from the Upper Paleolithic era spoke different languages,** it is unclear whether or not these languages were related to the larger proto-Indo-European language group from which later European languages would develop.

18. **In what is now modern-day Russia and Ukraine, people cultivated wild grains** like rye and wheat, which allowed them to produce their food rather than relying entirely on hunting and gathering.

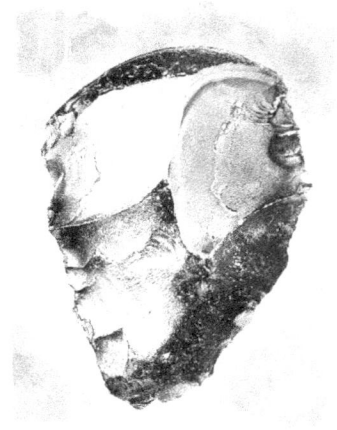

19. Toward the end of **the Upper Paleolithic Era** (around 12,000 BCE), some parts of **Europe experienced colder temperatures,** which limited the available resources like plants, animals, and water sources.

20. **Humans were forced to adopt a more settled lifestyle.** Farming became more common than hunting and gathering, but this process was accelerated during the Neolithic Revolution.

Mesolithic Period and Neolithic Revolution
(8000–4500 BCE)

Explore **twenty interesting facts about daily life during the Mesolithic period and the Neolithic Revolution.** We'll take a look at how people lived during these eras, from their homes to what they ate.

21. **Archaeologists call it the Mesolithic period, which means "Middle" Stone Age.** The Mesolithic period was between the Paleolithic (Old Stone Age) and Neolithic (New Stone Age) periods.

22. During this period, **people made their homes from materials like animal skins, reeds, branches, and clay** mixed with water to form walls that would keep out the wind and rain.

23. **Fishing was an important source of protein for many communities in Europe.** Some people had special boats that allowed them to fish more easily over larger areas of water.

24. **The Neolithic Revolution began around ten thousand years ago.** People started growing crops and keeping animals for food rather than relying solely on hunting and gathering.

25. **This period saw the emergence of the first permanent settlements in Europe,** as well as large-scale farming practices, which led to an increase in population density throughout regions like Britain and northern France.

26. **The Neolithic Revolution brought different advancements in technology,** such as the advent of polished axes in Europe. These tools could be used for chopping wood and cutting down trees faster than ever before.

27. **As populations increased, so did trade.** Goods could be exchanged between different areas and groups for things that weren't available locally, like metal and other raw materials.

28. By 4500 BCE (the end of this era), **societies had become much more complex.** Different social classes emerged due to increased wealth from trading or through military conquest.

29. **Ceramics were first produced during this period.** Pottery vessels served decorative and practical purposes in the home.

30. **The combination of farming and animal husbandry led to surplus yields,** which needed to be stored in newly developed granaries in order to preserve them for a long time.

31. **Religion became an important part of life.** It is believed that many religious ceremonies started taking place around this time in European history.

32. **Cattle were one type of livestock kept by people living in Europe at this time.** Cattle were valuable sources of protein, and their skins could be used for practical purposes.

33. **Archeological evidence suggests developments in the practice of herbalism – the use of plants as forms of medicine – during this period,** though such practices had emerged thousands of years earlier.

34. **It is believed the Neolithic Revolution spread to Europe from the Fertile Crescent in Mesopotamia,** where these developments occurred a couple thousand years prior.

35. **This meant that prominent crops from Southwest Asia were also introduced to Europe during this time, like barley and emmer.**

36. **The Neolithic Revolution saw the rise of monuments and towering stone structures called megaliths,** which were used as places for rituals, celebrations, or burials.

37. **Among the most well-known Neolithic megaliths in Europe are the Stonehenge in England and the Carnac Stones in northwestern France.**

38. **Artistic expression flourished during the Mesolithic period.** Cave paintings depicting animals or scenes from everyday life were created across Europe using natural pigments, such as red ochre.

39. **The domestication of sheep and goats for their wool and milk greatly impacted Europe's development during this era.** These animals provided food and materials from which to make clothing, which was important in cold climates.

40. **It is believed that women played important roles in their communities by gathering food, caring for children,** managing household tasks, and even participating in religious ceremonies alongside men.

Bronze Age
(3500–1200 BCE)

The Bronze Age in Europe was a remarkable time of innovation and growth. Tools and weapons were made from bronze for the first time, leading to increased mobility and trade. In this chapter, we will explore twenty interesting facts about the Bronze Age, including facts about writing systems and warfare.

41. **The Bronze Age was a time in Europe when people made tools and weapons out of bronze, an alloy of copper and tin.**

42. **Bronze tools were much stronger than the stone tools that had been used before.**

43. **The oldest known writing systems in Europe emerged in the Aegean. The Linear A, Cypro-Minoan, and Cretan hieroglyph writing systems developed in Europe** during the first half of the second millennium BCE.

44. **The oldest known writing system in Europe that has been fully deciphered is called Linear B,** which dates back to about 1400 BCE during the Late Bronze Age in Greece.

45. **The Linear B script was deciphered in 1952 and consists of more than eighty syllable signs,** as well as more than one hundred ideograms that denote objects in writing and cannot be pronounced phonetically.

46. **Bronze smelting gradually spread throughout Western Eurasia.** Some evidence indicates that it might have been independently developed multiple times at different places within the region.

47. **From about 3500 BCE, it spread gradually throughout Europe,** from southeastern parts such as the Aegean Islands, the Balkans, and the Caucasus to western Europe.

48. **The Bronze Age was a period of great social change in Europe.** New forms of government emerged, and large cities were built, such as Knossos on the island of Crete.

49. **Archaeologists have found evidence that some communities during the Bronze Age buried their dead in tombs filled with valuable objects like jewelry or weapons made from bronze.**

50. **The Bronze Age saw an expansion in trade and commerce** due to the increased availability of metal tools and weapons.

51. **Clear evidence of warfare has been found throughout Europe** from this era, suggesting that conflict was commonplace.

52. **Bronze swords were used by European armies during the Bronze Age.**

53. **Women played an important role in society.** They could be priestesses or even rulers! However, men tended to rule the most often.

54. **Bronze was used to produce jewelry and artwork like gold ornaments and decorated shields.**

55. **It is believed the first complex European civilizations started to emerge during the Bronze Age,** likely due to the technological and cultural advancements that made it possible to live sustainably in large communities.

56. **Initially, these civilizations were located around the Mediterranean Sea** because of the more favorable living conditions and proximity to other civilizations in Egypt and Mesopotamia.

57. **By the end of this era, the chariot was becoming an important part of warfare and transportation** due to its speed on rough terrain when compared with walking or riding horseback.

58. **Pottery production experienced rapid growth,** with vessels becoming much larger and more complexly decorated.

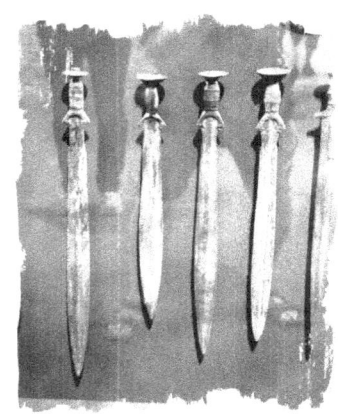

59. **The use of bronze tools allowed humans to do things like mine and build complex structures and weapons** that were much more efficient than previous versions.

60. **The Bronze Age ended when iron replaced bronze as the metal of choice** for tools and weapons, ushering in a new age known as the Iron Age.

The Rise of the Minoan Civilization
(c. 3000–1100 BCE)

This chapter will explore the incredible history of the Minoan civilization, one of the first major civilizations in Europe. We'll take a look at an impressive array of facts about their culture, beliefs, and arts. **Uncover why this ancient society had such a huge impact on later civilizations like ancient Greece and Rome.**

61. **The Minoan civilization is often considered the first civilization in Europe.** It began around 3000 BCE.

62. **The Minoans were mainly farmers who lived on islands off the coast of mainland Greece, such as Crete.**

63. **They built impressive palaces with large courtyards, storerooms, workshops, and private apartments for royalty or important people.** Minoan palaces have been found at **Knossos and Phaistos.**

64. **The Minos Palace on the island of Knossos,** for example, is a site that served both as a religious and an administrative center, and was not only used for royal residence – being a testament to **the sophisticated Minoan culture.**

65. **They developed the Linear A script,** which has still not been fully deciphered by modern scholars.

66. **Their culture is believed to have been based on maritime trade due to their location near the Mediterranean Sea.** They were connected to other civilizations, such as Egypt, Syria, and Anatolia.

67. **The Minoans had a rich art tradition that included pottery making, metalworking, and jewelry-making.** Many of these surviving artifacts are now housed in museums around the world.

68. **They were known for their beautiful frescoes and intricate relief designs** that depicted scenes of nature, people, and animals.

69. **The Minoans are believed to have invented true fresco,** a technique that results in the pigment becoming part of the wall.

70. **They believed in many gods, including ones that represented nature.** For instance, they believed snakes represented fertility and bulls for strength.

71. **They developed advanced architectural techniques, such as archways and columns to support the weight of buildings,** some of which reached up to three stories!

72. **The Minoan civilization is famous for having one of the oldest labyrinths ever built.** This winding maze full of secret passages and chambers is thought to have been located in Crete's Palace of Knossos.

73. **Unlike other ancient civilizations, women often held higher positions than men in society.** Some even served as priestesses at important religious sites like the Palace of Knossos.

74. **The Minoans built complex irrigation systems to bring fresh water into cities and surrounding areas,** which allowed them to develop and advance agricultural methods.

75. **They were skilled seafarers. Their ships even traveled as far away as Egypt and Syria!**

76. **The civilization was named after Minos, a figure in Greek mythology** who was a king of Crete and the son of Zeus and Europa.

77. **The Minoan civilization declined after c. 1450 BCE.** For the next few centuries, it would be dominated and eventually taken over politically and culturally by the Mycenaean civilization from mainland Greece.

78. **It is also thought the Minoan culture was destroyed by natural disasters,** such as earthquakes and volcanic eruptions, which caused massive destruction to their cities.

79. **In c. 1600 BCE, for example, the eruption of the Thera volcano is believed to have caused an ecological catastrophe in the region.**

80. **We know much more about this civilization today thanks to Sir Arthur Evans,** who discovered many artifacts during archaeological excavations between 1900 and 1930 CE.

Mycenaean Civilization
(1750–1050 BCE)

Discover the fascinating history of the Mycenaean civilization. We'll explore twenty interesting facts about their lifestyle, including how they were heavily influenced by the Minoan civilization.

81. **The Mycenaeans were an ancient civilization that lived during the Bronze Age in Greece** from around 1750 to 1050 BCE.

82. **While the Minoans lived on the Greek islands, the Mycenaeans lived mostly in mainland Greece.**

83. **Their culture was heavily influenced by the Minoan civilization.** Both civilizations shared similar styles of pottery, jewelry, and other artifacts, as well as religious rituals and customs.

84. **Because of this, the Mycenaean civilization is sometimes referred to as the successor of the Minoan civilization.**

85. **Scholars believe that Homer's epic stories, such as the Odyssey and the Iliad,** were inspired by actual events that took place during this period.

86. **Archaeologists have uncovered many tombs and sites throughout Greece belonging to Mycenaean rulers and nobles.** They have found various gold artifacts, weapons, and armor.

87. **The Mycenaeans were prolific traders with other nearby civilizations, such as Egypt, the Hittite Empire, and Anatolia.** They exchanged goods for precious metals like copper, bronze, and tin.

88. **When it comes to political organization, the Mycenae king, called the wanax, combined military, political, and religious roles. He ruled the Mycenean state.**

89. **Their economy was based largely on agriculture.** They grew wheat, barley, olives, and grapes to produce wine or olive oil that was exported around the Mediterranean region.

90. **Warfare played an essential role in their society.** Warriors would use chariots drawn by horses or oxen during battle. **The Mycenaeans** would be armed with swords, spears, or bows and arrows.

91. **Pottery from this period depicts scenes from daily life,** such as farmers working in the fields, fishermen out at sea catching their dinner, or people attending religious ceremonies.

92. **The Mycenaeans developed much of the ancient Greek mythology and worshiped gods such as Zeus, Poseidon, Artemis, and Hera.** Sacrifices were made to appease these deities.

93. **Their architecture was quite advanced for the period.** Large palaces with vaulted ceilings made from **stone blocks called megarons** could be found at nearly every major Mycenaean site in Greece!

94. **The archeological sites of Mycenae and Tiryns, located in the Peloponnese,** are the two places that contain the best evidence of this period, including ancient ruins that still stand strong today.

95. **The term "Mycenaean" is derived from the Greek city of Mycenae, one of their most powerful strongholds and home to legendary King Agamemnon,** the leader during the Trojan War.

96. **Agamemnon, as well as other figures from Mycenaean history, are believed to be half-real and half-legends.** These figures are often mentioned in mythological stories.

97. **The Mycenaeans made fine jewelry using gold, silver, and other precious stones like lapis lazuli or carnelian.**

98. **Their art and designs were characterized by geometric shapes, such as circles, triangles, spirals, and zigzags.**

99. **Mycenaean language was part of the larger Proto-Indo-European language family,** containing characteristics that were lost over time and did not emerge in the later Ancient Greek.

100. **The Mycenaean civilization eventually began to decline sometime around 1200 BCE during the Bronze Age Collapse.** This event is still mysterious, but many speculate that it was caused by natural disasters or even invasions from foreign tribes.

Ancient Greece
(800–146 BCE)

This chapter will dive into the captivating history of ancient Greece. We'll explore twenty interesting facts about their culture, beliefs, and government. **The Greeks laid some very important foundations;** it's time to take a look at how influential they were!

101. After the Bronze Age Collapse, the people who inhabited modern-day Greece, **the Aegean Islands, and parts of eastern Anatolia entered a period of decline called the Greek Dark Ages.**

102. **The people in these lands referred to themselves as Hellenes and the land they lived in as Hellas.** They spoke the same language and shared much of their culture, contributing to the formation of a common identity.

103. **However, ancient Greece was not a unified state or an empire.** Instead, ancient Greece consisted of many city-states, each with its own form of government.

104. **Two of the most city-states were Athens and Sparta. Athens had an early form of democracy, and Sparta was ruled by two kings.**

105. **The Greek city-states began to emerge after the end of the Greek Dark Ages,** beginning around 800 BCE.

106. **Over the next few centuries, the city-states rapidly developed the Greek culture and society.** Ancient Greece arguably became the most advanced civilization of its time.

107. **The Greeks believed in living a balanced life, with physical activity, education, religion, and art** all playing important roles in everyday life.

108. **They practiced science and mathematics,** leading to advances in astronomy, engineering, medicine, and more.

109. **Ancient Greek culture was spread through trade with other regions,** creating a cultural exchange that can still be seen in modern-day Europe and beyond.

110. **Some Greek city-states like Athens had a well-developed system of law courts** that allowed citizens to access justice without fear of punishment from rulers.

111. **Ancient Greece had an alphabet that was adapted from Phoenician traders.** It featured influences from earlier scripts of the region and, in its modified form, is still used for writing in Greek to this day.

112. **The Greeks worshiped gods like Zeus, Athena, Apollo, and Aphrodite.** These deities were made into statues and other artworks. The Greeks also had temples, like the Parthenon in Athens, which still stands today.

113. **The ancient Greeks built stadiums for sporting events** where thousands would come to watch competitions between athletes worldwide.

114. **In Olympia in 776 BCE, the first Olympic Games took place.** They would be held every four years for twelve centuries!

115. **Advances in political and social thought, as well as in philosophy,** helped create a complex Greek society that influenced neighboring civilizations.

116. **Ancient Greece is well known for its thinkers, such as Socrates, Plato, and Aristotle.** These men contributed greatly to the study of the world.

117. **Greek philosophers wrote about human nature, ethics, and government in books like the Republic.** These writings are still used today to understand politics.

118. **The Greeks created masterpieces of art, including sculptures depicting gods and heroes from mythology, pottery painted with beautiful scenes,** and intricate jewelry crafted out of gold or silver.

119. **Architects built theaters where plays were performed for large audiences.** Some famous ancient Greek playwrights include Sophocles and Euripides.

120. **Ancient Greece was the birthplace of Western civilization. Its ideas, art, language, and literature shaped much of Europe and even parts of Asia.**

The Greco-Persian Wars
(499—449 BCE)

The Greco-Persian Wars was a major conflict between the ancient Greek city-states and the Persian Empire. This section will explore twenty facts about this important conflict, such as why war broke out.

121. **The Greco-Persian Wars were a series of wars fought between the Greek city-states and the Persian Empire.** The wars started in 499 BCE and ended in 449 BCE.

122. **This conflict is also known as the Persian Wars or the Great War.** The battles in these wars took place both on land and at sea.

123. **At its peak, Persia stretched from the Balkan states in Europe to India and south to Egypt.** It was a powerful player in the Middle East.

124. **Two of the most powerful city-states at this time in ancient Greece were Athens and Sparta, exerting their influence on neighboring smaller city-states.** They led the Greek resistance against the Persians.

125. **The region of the Peloponnese was dominated by Sparta, a military powerhouse,** which founded the Peloponnesian League in the 6th century BCE – an alliance mainly consisting of the region's independent city-states.

126. **The initial cause of the war stemmed from disagreements over trading rights within Ionia** (modern-day Turkey).

127. **Persian rulers Darius I and Xerxes would try on different occasions to launch invasions into mainland Greece** and get the city-states to submit to Persian rule. However, these invasions would eventually end in failure.

128. **The Greeks won despite being outnumbered because they used clever tactics,** such as delaying the Persians long enough to gain help from their allies.

129. **One of the most famous battles in these wars was the Battle of Marathon, which took place in 490 BCE.** The Greek army defeated the invading Persian force by using superior strategy and tactics.

130. **The modern marathon was inspired by the Battle of Marathon. Pheidippides, Athens's greatest runner, is said to have run from Marathon to Athens to deliver news of the victory of the Battle of Marathon.** When he announced the victory, he fell down, dead.

131. **The Greeks' victories at sea were mainly due to their smaller but more agile ships** that could outmaneuver larger Persian vessels.

132. **Sparta was one of the main Greek forces that fought against Persia during this period.** Sparta was well known for its military tradition and well-trained hoplites.

133. **During the Greco-Persian Wars, a famous Athenian leader named Themistocles** used a naval strategy to defeat a much larger Persian fleet at Salamis in 480 BCE.

134. **The Battle of Thermopylae in 480 BCE is another battle from these wars that has become legendary.** The movie 300 was loosely based on the conflict. Three hundred Spartan warriors, seven hundred Thespians, and hundreds of helots stood against an overwhelming number of Persians. The Greeks were fought to the death.

135. **In 479 BCE, Greece experienced its greatest victory over the Persians at the Battle of Plataea** when 10,000 Greeks defeated 100,000 Persians led by Xerxes.

136. **In 478, Athens founded the Delian League, a confederation of Greek city-states with the purpose of fighting the Persian Empire.** The Delian League included many Greek islands in the Aegean, resulting in it emerging as the most powerful naval force in the region.

137. **The war ended when both sides agreed to end hostilities through the Peace of Callias in c. 449 BCE.** The peace granted autonomy to Ionian city-states and settlements in Asia Minor, with Persian ships being excluded from entering the Aegean.

138. **Following the conclusion of these wars,** Athens became one of the main powers in the ancient Mediterranean world.

139. **In the aftermath of the Greco-Persian Wars,** Greece experienced its golden age. This period saw art, literature, and philosophy flourish.

140. **The aftermath of the Greco-Persian Wars also saw the escalation between the two alliances led by Athens and Sparta,** concluding in the outbreak of the Peloponnesian War between the two sides in 431.

141. **This conflict lasted until 404 BCE and proceeded in a series of phases,** during which the two sides vied for hegemony and influence in the ancient Greek world.

142. **Spartans adopted an aggressive policy and attacked the Athenians and their allies** with the heavy hoplite units that were considered to have been among the best soldiers of the ancient world.

143. **Athenian strategy, on the other hand,** was containment on land and reliance on naval attacks and blockades, as **the Athenian-led Delian League** was superior in the sea.

144. **The Peloponnesian War ended in the defeat of Athens and its allies** in 404 BCE, with Sparta emerging as the new hegemon in ancient Greece for a time.

145. **About a hundred years after the conclusion of the Greco-Persian Wars, Alexander the Great from the Kingdom of Macedon** would unite almost all of Greece and end the Persian Empire.

Alexander the Great and the Hellenic League

This concise overview navigates through pivotal events, from post-Peloponnesian War turbulence to Philip II of Macedon's ambitions. Explore the extraordinary reign of **Alexander the Great**, whose conquests reshaped the ancient world, leaving behind a legacy of Hellenization.

146. After the end of **the Peloponnesian War**, Athens was briefly ruled by a group of oligarchs known as **the Thirty Tyrants.**

147. **The Thirty Tyrants were installed by Sparta** to keep the city-state under Spartan influence.

148. **The Thirty Tyrants were overthrown a year later.** Spartan dominance in the region was challenged by **the Corinthian War** (395–387 BCE).

149. During this war, **Athens, aided by the city-states of Corinth, Argos, and Thebes, fought Sparta.** They were unable to achieve a decisive victory, ultimately leading to the weakening of both sides.

150. **The Peace of Antalcidas was concluded in 387 BCE** after the Persian Empire intervened on the side of the allied city-states and aided them against the Spartans.

151. **After the conclusion of the war, the city-state of Thebes** was able to exploit the weakened state of Sparta and rebelled against Spartan hegemony in 378 BCE.

152. **Thebes was able to defeat Sparta in the Battle of Leuctra** in 371 BCE, leading to a brief period of Theban hegemony over Greece, which lasted until 362 BCE.

153. In 362, **the Battle of Mantinea** took place. Epaminondas, a leader who helped Thebes rise to power, died in the battle. This led to a decline in Theban power.

154. **Instability in the region resulted in significantly weaker Greek city-states** by the mid-4th century BCE compared to their state prior to the beginning of the Greco-Persian Wars.

155. **The instability also led to the rise of Panhellenic ideas among the Greeks,** preferring political unity instead of the current status quo of city-states.

156. **The Kingdom of Macedon, a Hellenistic kingdom located in the north centered around the city of Pella,** began to rise to power in the mid- to late 4th century BCE.

157. **Macedon had remained neutral for most of the wars in Greece** and was in a more powerful position to emerge as a dominant force in Greece by the end of the century.

158. **King Philip II of Macedon decided to impose his influence over the other city-states,** partly to unite them against the looming Persian threat.

159. **King Philip formed the League of Corinth, an alliance of city-states under Macedon.** It held its first council in Corinth after Philip's forces emerged victorious in the Battle of Chaeronea in 338 BCE against Thebes and Athens.

160. **The Macedonian king proposed a defensive alliance among the southern Greek city-states** (except for Sparta, which refused). He refused to impose his authority through military means.

161. **He was succeeded by his son and designated heir Alexander III,** who would come to be known as **Alexander the Great.** He would become one of the most accomplished rulers of all time.

162. **Alexander's first policy was to subdue the Greek city-states,** and he campaigned extensively during the first few years of his reign in the Balkans.

163. In 335 BCE, **Alexander decisively defeated the Thebans and destroyed the city of Thebes,** something that forced other city-states to submit to Alexander.

164. **Alexander was also able to secure the frontier provinces with Persian possessions** in Asia Minor for his war against the Achaemenids.

165. **Alexander was able to achieve a complete conquest of the vast Persian Empire** by the time of his unexpected death in 323 BCE.

166. **Alexander achieved decisive victories in the battles of Granicus** (334 BCE), **Issus** (333 BCE), **Tyre and Gaza** (332 BCE), and **Gaugamela** (331 BCE), which allowed him to overwhelm Persian resistance and claim Persian lands for himself.

167. **Entering victorious in Persian satrapies in Asia Minor, the Levant, Egypt, and Iran, Alexander was accepted as the new leader** and emerged as one of the most powerful figures of all of antiquity.

168. **Alexander's conquests reached as far as the Indus River in the east.**

169. **Alexander died in Babylon in 323 BCE.** It is not known for sure what caused his death, but most scholars believe he died of typhoid fever or some other illness.

170. **Alexander's empire disintegrated soon after his death.** The territories he had gained were split among his generals in **the Wars of the Diadochi.**

171. **His conquests caused massive sociocultural shifts throughout the ancient world.** It resulted in the influx of Greek settlers in these lands and a subsequent process of Hellenization, the spread of Greek culture and traditions.

172. **Ancient Greek became the lingua franca of the ancient world.** Greek customs were fused with rich local traditions to produce unique regional variations for the next few hundred years.

173. **The resulting Hellenistic period was marked by great achievements in arts, science, and philosophy.**

174. **The polities that succeeded Alexander's empire** eventually became too unstable and were conquered by the Romans.

175. **The ancient Greek world left behind an astonishing legacy** that stands as a testament to the importance of this era in European and world history.

The Roman Republic
(509–27 BCE)

This chapter will explore the incredible history of the Roman Republic, another early great civilization in Europe. We'll take a look at twenty-five interesting facts about their government, religions, engineering feats, and more!

176. **The city of Rome was legendarily founded in 753 BCE by twin brothers named Remus and Romulus.**

177. **The Roman civilization quickly grew from the city of Rome,** occupying most of central Italy by the 6th century BCE.

178. **The Romans battled other people groups living in the peninsula,** including the Etruscans, who were mostly concentrated in the north, and Greek city-states in the south.

179. **The Romans spoke the Latin language, which was originally a dialect spoken in the Latium region in central Italy.**

180. **Through military victories over their neighbors,** the Romans would emerge as the most dominant power in Italy. **The Latin culture** was later spread around other parts of the world by the Romans.

181. **Unlike ancient Greece, Rome was initially a kingdom. Its last king, Tarquinius Superbus,** was overthrown around 509 BCE, and a republic was established.

182. **The word "republic" comes from the Latin res publica, meaning "public affair."** It is a state where political power is supposed to be held by the people.

183. **The Romans were greatly influenced by the Greek culture and way of life.** They adopted a political system similar to that of the Greeks, as well as their complex system of gods.

184. **The Roman gods governed over different aspects of life, like war, agriculture, or death, much like the Greek gods.** The Roman gods corresponded to the Greek gods, except most had different names. For example, Zeus was called Jupiter.

185. **The Romans established a legislative branch called the Senate,** which was composed of tens and then hundreds of citizens who were chosen by the consuls and served for life as magistrates.

186. **The consuls were the two leaders of the Roman Republic. They served one-year terms.** They had a special power called veto, which meant they could stop their colleague from doing something if it was a bad idea.

187. **The Roman Republic was divided into two classes: the patricians, who were wealthy landowners and business owners,** and the plebeians, who were commoners or peasants who worked on farms or in businesses owned by the patricians.

188. **The Roman Republic was divided into different provinces,** which were ruled by governors who had been appointed by the Senate in Rome.

189. **The earliest written legislation of Rome was the Twelve Tables, which was first promulgated in c. 450 BCE.** They reconfirmed the class distinctions between the plebeians and the patricians and recognized the rights of each.

190. **The Romans were great engineers.** They built roads, some of which still stand today. They also built aqueducts to move water from place to place, bridges across rivers, and walls around their cities for protection against enemies.

191. **All citizens of the Roman Republic had certain rights, including the right to vote on laws and elect officials who would lead them.**

192. **Not everyone could be a citizen. You had to be male, and both your parents had to be Roman.** Later on, the senators and even emperors would grant citizenship to people living in the Roman Empire.

193. **Gladiator fights were popular entertainment among Romans.** These fighters fought each other using weapons like swords or spears at events held in large arenas.

194. **The Romans built one of the first versions of a sewer system to remove waste from public areas in their cities.**

195. **Romans paid a lot of attention to learning and science,** much like the Greeks, leaving behind a rich cultural legacy.

196. **Rome was notorious for its professional military,** which was one of the key reasons behind its formation as a powerful state.

197. **The Roman legions created complex formations called tortoises,** which allowed the soldiers to move around on battlefields while being protected and having access to their weapons during battle if needed.

198. **The ancient Romans had many different types of soldiers, including cavalry** (horse-mounted warriors), **infantry** (soldiers who fought on foot), **and auxiliaries** (non-Roman citizens who served as soldiers).

199. **While the Romans did not invent concrete,** they were the first to use it for most of their construction projects, which included amphitheaters, temples, and aqueducts.

200. **After the establishment of the republic, Rome expanded its territories,** emerging as masters of Italy, southern Iberia, and the North African coast. It would later become one of the greatest empires in world history.

The Roman Empire
(27 BCE–476 CE)

The Roman Empire is one of the most iconic and influential periods in all of history. Spanning from 27 BCE to 476 CE, this period saw vast expansion and a flourishing culture. Let's explore twenty facts about the Roman Empire!

201. **By the 1st century BCE, Rome had expanded rapidly, taking over Greece and parts of Anatolia.** It also controlled Iberia and North Africa.

202. **The Senate had to govern a very large territory,** which was practically impossible. Local commanders and generals held a lot of power in the Roman provinces.

203. During the 1st century BCE, **the Roman Republic suffered from internal conspiracies and civil wars.** The generals continued expanding their power.

204. **Julius Caesar, one of the most powerful generals who conquered Gaul,** marched his forces into Rome. He took control of the republic in 45 BCE.

205. **Julius Caesar was assassinated in 44 BCE by the senators.** Different factions formed, but Julius Caesar's adopted son and successor, Augustus (formerly known as Octavian), declared himself emperor in 27 BCE by order of the Senate.

206. **Augustus was granted the title of princeps** (first citizen) and became the de facto ruler of all of Rome.

207. **The Julio-Claudian dynasty, founded by Augustus,** included emperors such as **Tiberius, Caligula, Claudius, and Nero.**

208. **The Senate still existed, but it did not have that much power.** Augustus reduced the number of senators from nine hundred to six hundred.

209. At its height, **the Roman Empire stretched from Britain to North Africa and parts of Asia Minor** (modern-day Turkey).

210. **During the Pax Romana** (the Roman Peace), which lasted from 27 BCE to 180 CE, there was stability in the Roman Empire, although wars with outside forces still occurred.

211. From the late 1st to the 2nd century CE, Rome was ruled by five consecutive emperors, who are sometimes referred to as the Five Good Emperors.

212. This term was coined by Niccolo Machiavelli in the 16th century to describe the period of stability under the emperors Nerva, Trajan, Hadrian, Antoninus Pius, and Marcus Aurelius.

213. Machiavelli claimed that the Roman Empire prospered because the emperors chose their heirs; the throne wasn't inherited at that time.

214. Trajan, emperor from 98 to 117 CE, expanded the Roman Empire to its greatest territorial extent, including the conquest of Dacia (modern-day Romania) and parts of Mesopotamia.

215. Marcus Aurelius, who reigned from 161 to 180 CE, was not only one of the most successful emperors of Rome but also made a name for himself due to his contributions to the philosophy of Stoicism.

216. His Meditations, a series of personal writings in Koine Greek that were composed by the emperor for his own personal use, has become one of the best-selling philosophical books.

217. Latin became the common language that united all people living under the rule of Rome, which helped them stay connected.

218. The Crisis of the Third Century (235–284 CE) was a period of political, military, and economic instability characterized by frequent changes of emperors and invasions by external tribes.

219. In order to better control the vast territories of the Empire, Emperor Diocletian introduced a system called the Tetrarchy in 286 CE.

220. The Tetrarchy was a division of Roman lands into two administrative units of East and West, each ruled by a separate augustus. Some later emperors became rulers of both parts.

221. **Diocletian also introduced several other administrative and economic reforms that helped stabilize the situation of the empire during the late third century.**

222. **The division of the empire was made final in 395 upon the death of Emperor Theodosius I,** the last emperor of united Rome. His sons, Honorius and Arcadius, emerged as the emperors of the Western and Eastern Roman Empires, respectively.

223. **Emperor Constantine the Great,** who ruled from 306 to 337 CE, constructed a new imperial residence at **the Bosphorus Strait.** This city, Constantinople, became the capital of the Eastern Roman Empire.

224. **Christianity was initially persecuted by the emperors. Nero** and others were infamous for their brutal treatment and hatred toward the Christians.

225. **Constantine the Great legalized Christianity with the Edict of Milan** in 313 CE, which ended the persecution of Christians in the empire.

226. **In 380 CE, Emperor Theodosius declared Christianity the official state religion,** something that was followed by a gradual rooting out of Roman pagan practices throughout the empire's territories.

227. **Hadrian's Wall was built by the Romans in 122 CE** to protect against the barbarians in northern England and Scotland.

228. In 475 CE, **Romulus Augustus became the last emperor of the Western Roman Empire.** His reign ended a year later when Rome was invaded by the barbarian general Odoacer.

229. After 476 CE, **power shifted away from Rome.** Smaller kingdoms were formed that controlled different sections of Europe.

230. **The fall of the Roman Empire led to the Middle Ages,** a period in Europe when there was less centralized government and more reliance on local rulers for protection.

The Migration Period
(375–700 CE)

This chapter will explore the Migration Period in Europe, a period of intense movement and change. We'll take a look at twenty interesting facts about how these migrations influenced Europe.

231. **The Migration Period refers to a time of large-scale westward migrations of different eastern European tribal peoples.**
232. **The Migration Period resulted in barbarian invasions in the lands of the Roman Empire.** Some of these tribes, such as the Ostrogoths and Visigoths, were involved in the fall of the Western Roman Empire in 476.
233. **It is hard to know for sure how many people migrated during this time,** but estimates don't go above 750,000.
234. **Germanic tribes migrated into northern and western Europe from their homeland near the Black Sea region in eastern Europe.**

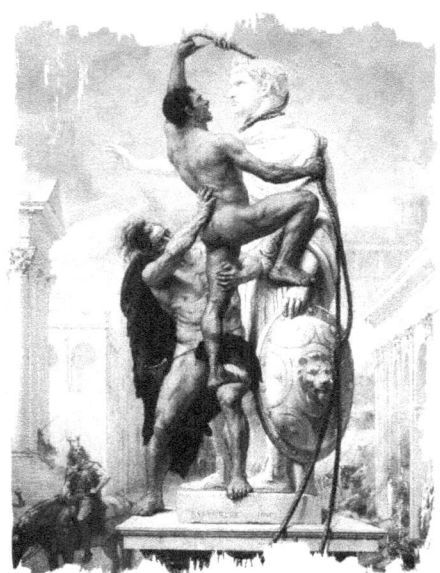

235. **These tribes included the Visigoths, Franks, Vandals, and Angles.** They invaded Roman territories in Italy, Gaul, Iberia, and even North Africa.
236. **Romans referred to all non-Roman peoples as barbarians,** and they implemented different policies in dealing with them.

237. **Although the Roman Empire conquered many barbarian territories,** it sometimes allowed neighboring barbarians to come and settle in lands controlled by Rome.
238. **Rome was sacked four times by the barbarians. The Visigoth attack on Rome** in 410 is often viewed as the beginning of the end of the Roman Empire.
239. **The Roman forces had a hard time controlling the barbarians.** Rome was also dealing with internal instability, civil wars, and an economic crisis.

240. **One of the major reasons the barbarians started moving westward was because of the Huns.** They made devastating attacks on people living in eastern Europe, forcing them to move out of the region.

241. **In 476, after about two centuries of dealing with large-scale barbarian invasions, Germanic King Odoacer deposed the last Western Roman emperor.** The rest of the empire disintegrated very quickly.

242. **The migrating tribes settled in different former Roman provinces and started to establish state-like formations** that were separate from each other.

243. **The Eastern Roman Empire was relatively unaffected by barbarian invasions and managed to survive the Migration Period intact.**

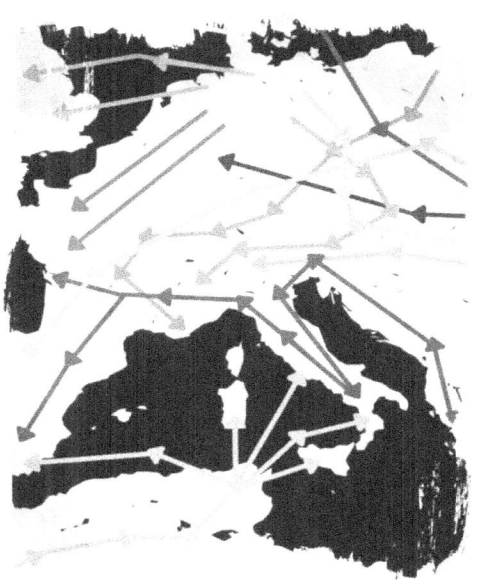

244. **The Migration Period led to the collapse of the Roman Latin culture** and the rise in the prominence of Germanic cultures.

245. **The new rulers tried to adopt former Roman customs and traditions to legitimize themselves as new leaders,** though this was only partially successful.

246. **Christianity strengthened these local authorities.** They used religious doctrine to control populations.

247. **The barbarian invasions led to a fragmentation of political authority, as individual leaders grew more powerful than before.** Local rulers became increasingly influential within their regions.

248. By 568, **most of the Germanic tribes had settled down in their new homelands.** The period of migration slowed down significantly.

249. **It is believed the Migration Period helped give rise to modern nation-states** by creating distinct ethnic and linguistic boundaries in Europe.

250. **The Migration Period saw a decline in trade and commerce as people moved away from cities,** resulting in economic instability throughout Europe.

The Early Middle Ages
(476–1000 CE)

The Early Middle Ages, sometimes called the Dark Ages, was a time of great transformation. This chapter will explore twenty fascinating facts about this era in history, from the spread of Christianity to technological advances. Let's see what this era was all about!

251. **The Early Middle Ages, which is part of the medieval period,** lasted from 476 to 1000 CE in Europe.
252. **This period is also known as the "Dark Ages"** because learning and culture declined due to invasions from groups like the Vikings, Muslims, and Magyars (Hungarians).
253. Many historians today dislike using **the term "Dark Ages" because it implies Europe was culturally stagnant during this time,** which was not the case
254. **The fall of the Western Roman Empire is traditionally seen as the beginning of the Early Middle Ages.**
255. **Overall, the Early Middle Ages was a time of instability and uncertainty in Europe as new states were formed on the remnants of the old Roman Empire.**

256. **Feudalism became a popular political and economic system during this time. People gave their loyalty to lords** in exchange for protection and land rights.

257. **Christianity spread throughout Europe, eventually replacing other religions, like the Norse religion.** It took centuries for Christianity to be accepted by most of a people group.
258. **The Anglo-Saxons converted relatively quickly to Christianity.** Most Anglo-Saxons were practicing Christians roughly a century after it had been introduced to England!
259. **The Roman Church saw itself as the symbolic successor to the Roman Empire.** It gained power and wealth during the medieval period.
260. **The church sent missionaries to different parts of Europe to spread Christianity and convert the pagan rulers.** One of the most missionaries was Saint Augustine, who brought Christianity to England in 597.

261. **The people built churches and cathedrals, which became important social centers for their communities.** People could gather there to worship or trade goods with each other at markets nearby.

262. **Monasteries became popular centers for learning in medieval Europe. Monks helped spread Christianity.** They were known for being pious and austere individuals.

263. **The Franks adopted the Latin language after they conquered Gaul** (modern-day France) around 500 CE. They made it the official language of administration and culture in the western European states.

264. **During the Early Middle Ages, people used Roman numerals** to keep track of numbers instead of the modern-day Arabic numerals that we use today.

265. **The Franks unified parts of Europe during the Carolingian Empire** (800–843), which was later dissolved due to internal disputes and fragmentation of political power.

266. In the 5th century, **the Angles, Saxons, and Jutes invaded Britain.** These people jointly became known as **the Anglo-Saxons.** They established their own language, Old English, which later developed into modern English!

267. **The Anglo-Saxon migration into Britain forced the local Brittonic peoples to move to the peripheries of the British Isles;** their societies survived in parts of Wales, Ireland, and Scotland.

268. Around 800 CE, **knights emerged due to feudalism.** They were part-time soldiers responsible for protecting their lord's castle or estate from invaders.

269. **The Early Middle Ages saw significant technological developments,** including improved horse harnesses and stirrups, heavy plows, and horseshoes, as well as more efficient crop rotation techniques.

270. **The Reconquista was launched by the Christians in 722** in hopes of reclaiming Iberia from the Muslim conquerors.

The Byzantine Empire
(330—1453 CE)

Explore the impressive history of the Byzantine Empire with these twenty-five interesting facts! From its founding to its fall, discover how this rich culture blended religions, languages, and art throughout Europe, Africa, and Asia.

271. **The Eastern Roman Empire, also known as the Byzantine Empire, was founded in the 4th century by Emperor Constantine I.** It lasted until 1453—about one thousand years after the fall of the Western Roman Empire!

272. **The name comes from the old Greek city of Byzantium,** which served as the site for the empire's capital, Constantinople.

273. **Constantinople was the center of Europe during the Middle Ages.** It was the largest and the richest city, with walls that were about forty feet high.

274. **At the time of its split from the Western Roman Empire,** the Byzantine Empire controlled lands in the Balkans, Anatolia, the Near East, and Egypt. It was far richer and more powerful than its western counterpart.

275. **The Byzantine Empire considered itself the rightful successor of Rome after its fall.** Many attempts were made to assert Byzantine authority in Europe during the Middle Ages.

276. **Justinian I, who reigned from 527 to 565, was able to take control of parts of Italy,** North Africa, and Iberia.

277. **Justinian is remembered as the ruler who tried to restore the borders of the old Roman Empire.** He is also remembered for his code of laws, which influenced many European states later on.

278. **Empress Theodora, Justinian's wife, was very influential.** She recognized the rights of women and used her influence to pass religious and social reforms.

279. **Despite Justinian's efforts, the Byzantine Empire was unable to assert its dominance over the rest of Europe.** The cultural differences between the Byzantine Empire and post-Roman western Europe would grow.

280. **The Byzantine Empire is known for its unique blend of cultures and religions,** but it was primarily a Greek state.

281. **Byzantine citizens spoke a form of Greek called Byzantine Greek,** though they also knew Latin.

282. **The majority of the territories the Byzantine Empire controlled had been Hellenized during the heyday of ancient Greece and with the conquests of Alexander the Great.**

283. **A series of controversial events would lead to the "official" split of the Christian Church in 1054.** The Great Schism saw the formation of the Western Roman Catholic Church and the Eastern Orthodox Church.

284. **The two churches would emerge as rivals,** and both would try to convert pagans to their own version of Christianity.

285. **Russia adopted Christianity from the Byzantine Empire in 988 CE,** which is why the Russian Orthodox Church follows similar religious traditions today.

286. **Islam's rise in the 7th century weakened the Byzantine Empire politically.** The invading Arab armies conquered many Byzantine lands in the Near East and Egypt.

287. **Still, up until about the 11th century, the Byzantine Empire continued to be very powerful.** It was known for its great military and wealthy economy.

288. **The Byzantine Empire was known for its impressive architecture,** including famous basilicas like **the Hagia Sophia in Constantinople.**

289. **The Byzantines had a powerful navy that was able to protect their coasts and control the Mediterranean Sea.**

290. **The Byzantines were known for using Greek fire (the precursor to napalm) during battle,** which could be projected at enemy ships or onto land.

291. **The empire started to enter a period of decline with the arrival of the Turkic peoples from central Asia,** who conducted military campaigns in Byzantine lands.

292. **The Seljuk Turks took over much of Anatolia by the 13th century.**

293. **In 1254, Constantinople was sacked by the Crusading Christian forces, weakening the empire even more.**

294. **The Ottoman Turks emerged as the new rival to Constantinople** in the 14th century. **They defeated the Byzantine armies** time and time again.

295. **Constantinople's walls helped protect it from invaders multiple times. However, the city fell in 1453 when Ottoman forces** conquered the city after a fifty-three-day siege.

Viking Invasions
(790– 1066 CE)

Explore the remarkable history of the Vikings and their impact on Europe in this section! We will look at twenty fascinating facts about how they lived, their famous leaders, and some of their major gods.

296. **The Vikings came from Scandinavia.** They were prominent from the 8th to the 11th century.

297. **The Vikings were seafaring warrior Scandinavians.** Most of them farmed for a living but raided in the off-season.

298. **Their longboats were made out of wood. Their ships were called drakkars.** They were designed to travel shallow rivers and over open ocean. The Vikings could carry them overland if they had to.

299. **Viking warriors often went on voyages called raids.** They invaded many different parts of Europe in search of treasure, land, and power.

300. **The word "Viking" is derived from an Old Norse phrase meaning "pirate raid."**

301. **In 790 CE, they raided a monastery off the coast of England.** This is traditionally seen as the start of the Viking Age.

302. **Some coastal towns built walls around them for defense against raids,** but few were able to withstand the full force of the vicious Viking attacks.

303. **Although Vikings are often depicted wearing helmets with horns, there is no evidence to support that they wore helmets like this.** The helmets they wore were very simple.

304. **The Vikings were well known for their brave and bold attitude in battle. Legend says that the Vikings had berserkers,** men who would go into a trance-like state and fight until the death.

305. **One of the most famous Viking leaders was Ragnar Lodbrok** (also spelled Lothbrok). He raided Paris in 845. **He was eventually killed by King Aella** (also spelled as Aelle) of Northumbria in England.

306. **The Vikings were known for their intricate woodworking and metalwork.** They were also known for creating weapons like swords.

307. **They established trading routes all over Europe.** They first focused on regions in the Baltic Sea but later expanded to the Mediterranean.

308. **While most people think that only men could be Vikings, women could too.** There were not as many female Vikings, but there is evidence they might have taken part in raids.

309. **Most women played important roles at home, like running farms or businesses while their husbands were away at sea.** Some took advisor roles and helped plan raids.

310. **The Norse pantheon included Odin** (the god of war and wisdom), **Thor** (the god of thunder), **Loki** (the god of mischief), and **Freya** (the goddess of love).

311. **The Vikings had their own language called Old Norse.** Although it is no longer spoken today, elements of it can be found in the North Germanic languages.

312. **They believed in a place called Valhalla,** where brave warriors went after they died in battle. There, they would feast with Odin in the afterlife.

313. **Vikings were very superstitious people.** They believed that trolls, elves, dragons, and sea monsters existed.

314. **During this period, the Vikings left behind many stories in their poetry, songs, and art,** which have been passed down for hundreds of years.

315. **To this day, we celebrate Viking culture with festivals, movies, and books about them.** Two of the best examples of this are the TV show Vikings and the comic books and movies about Thor.

The Reconquista
(722–1492)

The Reconquista saw multiple Christian military campaigns aimed at reclaiming Iberia from Islamic rule. These twenty-five facts will shed some light on this turbulent period in European history.

316. **The Reconquista is the name given to a series of Christian military campaigns against the Islamic realms** in Iberia during the Middle Ages between 718 and 1492.

317. **Iberia had been conquered during the initial stage of Islamic expansion by the emerging Umayyad Caliphate** at the beginning of the 8th century.

318. **They destroyed the Visigothic Kingdom, which had ruled Iberia since the late 5th century,** and established an Islamic caliphate.

319. **The Christian Europeans saw this as a threat.** They began a series of military operations to reclaim the lands they believed had been unjustly lost to the Muslims.

320. **Visigothic elites fled to the north of the Iberian Peninsula, establishing the Kingdom of Asturias.** They saw themselves as the rightful claimants of the lands held by the Muslims.

321. **In 718 or 722, the Asturian armies defeated the Muslims at the Battle of Covadonga,** an event that is considered to be the beginning of the Reconquista.

322. **Up until the early 11th century, the Caliphate of Córdoba was the major Islamic political entity in Iberia,** controlling most of modern-day Spain and Portugal.

323. **The Caliphate of Córdoba was unsuccessful in trying to subdue Christian resistance.** It disintegrated into smaller Islamic polities due to internal conflicts.

324. **In the year 910, under the leadership of King Alfonso III, the Kingdom of Asturias was reorganized into the Kingdom of León,** having gained a significant chunk of territory in central Iberia.

325. **Other Christian kingdoms, such as Castile, Navarre, and Galicia,** would also emerge, taking the fight to the Muslims and gradually pushing them back.

326. **These Christian kingdoms were not always allies with each other.** They often strategically chose their partners to gain more territory and even went to war with each other.

327. **The period between the 11th and 13th centuries saw significant advances in the Reconquista,** with key victories such as the capture of Toledo in 1085 by Alfonso VI of León and Castile.

328. **The Christian world supported the efforts of the Iberian kingdoms during the Reconquista, with Pope Alexander III** sanctioning a war effort in 1064 to attack the Muslim city of Barbastro, which ended in a Christian victory.

329. **Pope Urban II, who called for the First Crusade in 1095, encouraged the Reconquista in Iberia,** offering spiritual rewards to those who participated in the fight to reclaim Christian territories.

330. **Another important Christian victory came at the Battle of Las Navas de Tolosa in 1212,** in which the combined Castilian, Leonese, Navarrese, and Portuguese forces defeated the army of the Muslim Almohad dynasty in Andalusia.

331. **From the 12th to the 13th century, Christians were aided in their efforts by the newly established Catholic military orders in Iberia,** whose mission was to fight in the name of Christianity against its enemies.

332. **Orders, such as the Knights Templar and the Knights of Santiago,** proved to be extremely valuable, often taking control of key fortifications and contributing professional soldiers to Iberian armies.

333. The Iberians were also aided by the Crusaders on several occasions, most importantly in 1147 during the siege of Lisbon, which greatly strengthened the position of the Kingdom of Portugal.

334. The fall of Granada in 1492 marked the end of Muslim rule in Iberia.

335. The Catholic monarchs Isabella I of Castile and Ferdinand II of Aragon completed the Reconquista.

336. After the completion of the Reconquista, the victorious Christian kingdoms began to spread their own customs and traditions that were fused with local Muslim practices that had developed in Iberia since the 8th century.

337. The Reconquista had economic consequences, as the reconquered territories brought new resources, trade routes, and agricultural lands under Christian control.

338. The Reconquista led to major demographic changes, as the Muslim population of the peninsula was slowly assimilated into Christian kingdoms. Many chose to leave, while others were forcefully expelled under the new rulers.

339. In 1492, as many as 200,000 Castilian and Aragonese Jews, as a result of the Alhambra Decree, were expelled.

340. Christian rulers forced their new subjects to convert to Christianity, a process that was accelerated by the Spanish Inquisition.

Charlemagne
(r. 768–814 CE)

Charlemagne was one of the most important rulers in European history. Let's discover the impact he made with these twenty-five facts about his reign and life.

341. **Charlemagne, or Charles the Great, was the son of King Pepin the Short,** who founded **the Carolingian Empire.**

342. **Charlemagne became the king of the Franks in 768. He would become the sole ruler of the Franks** after his co-ruler, his brother, died in 771.

343. **The Carolingian line, founded by Charlemagne's father and bearing the name of the eventual emperor,** replaced the ruling Frankish Merovingian dynasty.

344. **Charlemagne continued his father's policies, forging good relations with the Roman Church,** expanding his kingdom at the expense of the German pagans, and spreading Christianity.

345. **As a wise king and a great warrior, he conquered much of western and central Europe.**

346. **He defeated the Lombards in 774. These Germanic peoples had taken over much of Italy in the 6th century.** Charlemagne granted many of their lands to the Roman Church.

347. **He also launched an invasion of Spain,** which had become Muslim after the Arabs invaded in the 7th and the beginning of the 8th century.

348. **Charlemagne's only military defeat came at the hands of the Muslims** (known as the Moors) in the Battle of Roncevaux Pass in 778.

349. **Charlemagne waged wars in what is now modern-day Germany,** where he expelled the pagan peoples and spread Christianity.

350. **He played a major role in bringing Christianity to many parts of Europe,** which united Europe after centuries of division.

351. **He would sometimes use cruel tactics to get people to convert.** For example, he told the Saxons to either be baptized in the Christian faith or die.

352. **During the infamous Massacre of Verden, for example,** Charlemagne executed thousands of Saxons who refused to convert to Christianity in October of 782.

353. **He conquered much of modern-day western Germany.** He moved his capital to the German city of Aachen, where he would eventually be buried in 814.

354. **Charlemagne reunified much of western Europe.** He would be recognized as the first emperor of Europe after the fall of the Roman Empire.

355. **Pope Leo III crowned Charlemagne in Rome on Christmas Day in 800, granting him the title of the emperor of the Romans.** This move upset the Byzantine Empire, which saw itself as the continuation of the Roman Empire.

356. **His coronation marked the beginning of what is now known as the Holy Roman Empire,** although it would be several centuries until the Holy Roman Empire had a stable successive rule.

357. **Soon after being crowned emperor, Charlemagne** made sure that each region he ruled had laws in place so they could govern themselves better according to their needs.

358. **He established schools across Europe to educate students on religion,** administration, economics, and other subjects.

359. **For centuries, no ruler would be able to control as much territory in western Europe as Charlemagne,** something that is a testament to his incredible achievements.

360. **He also created the first successful system of taxation in Europe since the fall of Rome,** something that would be used for centuries afterward.

361. **His prosperous reign marked the beginning of what is known as the Carolingian Renaissance,** a period of great cultural and intellectual revival after the fall of Rome.

362. **Carolingian art, for example, was produced in religious institutions of Charlemagne and his heirs,** and was the highest form of Christian art in all of Europe at the time.

363. **He is nicknamed the "Father of Europe"** due to his impressive accomplishments in reuniting Europe.

364. **He was succeeded by his son Louis the Pious. The Carolingian Empire** would then be split by Charlemagne's grandchildren, which led to its demise.

365. **The successive states, East and West Francia, eventually evolved into the Holy Roman Empire and France during the later Middle Ages.**

The High Middle Ages in European History
(1000–1350 CE)

We'll take a look at twenty-five interesting facts about Europe's economy, culture, technology, and more during the High Middle Ages. Let's discover what made this era so impactful!

366. **The High Middle Ages were a period of growth and progress for Europe's economy and population.** Europe's population grew from about forty million to a little over seventy million people!

367. **During this period, political and social structures in Europe started to stabilize after the instability of the Early Middle Ages,** with new kingdoms forming all over the continent.

368. **The Carolingian Empire would be split with the Treaty of Verdun in the 9th century,** leading to the eventual establishment of the Kingdom of France and the Holy Roman Empire.

369. **William the Conqueror was a Norman ruler who conquered England in 1066 CE.** This event is known as the Norman Conquest.

370. **The English monarchy would develop over the next few centuries, with the turning point coming in 1215 when King John I in England signed the Magna Carta,** which guaranteed certain rights to citizens, such as trial by jury.

371. **The first universities were formed during the High Middle Ages. These institutions taught Latin grammar,** rhetoric, astronomy, music theory, and medicine, among other subjects.

372. **The first university in Europe was the University of Bologna.** It was established in 1088 and is still operating today.

373. **The Crusades were fought by Europeans in an attempt to reclaim control over Jerusalem and other areas that had been conquered by Muslim forces centuries earlier.** The First Crusade started in 1096, and the last official Crusade took place in 1271.

374. **The High Middle Ages saw the rise of powerful monarchs, such as King Philip II of France and Richard I of England.** These rulers were able to extend their power over large areas.

375. **Christianity continued to spread throughout Europe,** reaching eastern Europe and Scandinavia by the 10th century.

376. **In fact, it was during this time that Christianity became an essential part of Europe,** thanks to the prior efforts of Charlemagne and the quick Christianization of central and eastern European peoples during the Late and High Middle Ages.

377. **The Magyar peoples organized their own kingdom, the Kingdom of Hungary,** by the year 1000. They adopted Christianity.

378. **Towns began to develop rapidly, and trade increased between cities across Europe.**

379. **An early form of banking emerged in the Italian city-states during this period because of increased merchant activity and the accumulation of wealth.** The Bank of Venice would officially be established in 1587.

380. **Military technology improved greatly. Knights wore heavy suits of armor made with metal plates joined together with rivets or leather straps.** These suits of armor could weigh up to sixty pounds!

381. **Gothic architecture became popular across Europe during the 12th century.** This style is known for its large stained glass windows and tall spires reaching up toward the sky.

382. **The High Middle Ages was one of the most politically turbulent and violent periods of European history.** Many destructive wars, such as the Hundred Years' War between England and France, were fought during this time.

383. **The invention of the mechanical clock improved navigation,** making it possible to measure time more accurately than ever before.

384. **During this period, many religious orders, such as the Franciscans and Dominicans, were founded.** They sought to spread Christianity around Europe.

385. **Greater scientific knowledge was gained through translations of works from Arab scholars into Latin,** which brought about a revolution in European medicine and science.

386. **Marco Polo is thought to have traveled to China sometime in the 13th century.** He brought back tales of exotic lands filled with spices and silks, helping fuel the growth of trade between the East and the West.

387. **Literature flourished during this era. Some famous authors include Geoffrey Chaucer,** who wrote The Canterbury Tales; Dante Alighieri, who wrote the Divine Comedy; and Thomas Aquinas, who wrote the Summa Theologica.

388. **Guilds started to be formed during the High Middle Ages.** These organizations helped protect workers' rights and regulate trade between cities.

389. **In the middle of the 14th century, Europe was ravaged by the outbreak of the bubonic plague.** It was known as the Great Plague, but we know it better as the Black Death.

390. **The Black Death is thought to have caused the deaths of about a third of Europe's population.** It greatly set back technological, cultural, and social developments.

The Renaissance
(14th–17th Centuries)

The Renaissance was a period of profound cultural, artistic, and scientific changes that swept across Europe from the 14th to the 17th century. This section will explore twenty-five interesting facts about one of the most influential periods in European history.

391. **The Renaissance was a period in European history that lasted from around the late 14th to the 17th century.** It marked an era of cultural revival in art, literature, architecture, and other aspects of life.

392. **Italy was at the heart of this movement,** with cities like Florence playing an important role in its development.

393. **The Renaissance followed a period of great instability and upheaval in Europe, known as the Crisis of the Late Middle Ages,** a series of events that caused political and socioeconomic collapse during the 13 and 14th centuries.

394. **During the Renaissance, new ideas emerged, such as humanism,** which focused on humans instead of God or fate as being responsible for their actions and destiny.

395. **Many of the ancient Roman and Greek texts that had been lost** or had only been accessible to the clergy were slowly rediscovered during the Renaissance.

396. **The rediscovery of ancient texts ushered in a period of great learning,** which manifested itself in almost all fields of life.

397. **The word "Renaissance" means "rebirth."** The term refers to the rebirth of ancient Greek and Roman ideas.

398. **Several wealthy families from Italy emerged as patrons of up-and-coming artists,** most prominently the Florentine Medici family – which financed the projects of such artists as Michelangelo.

399. **During this era, artists began using techniques like perspective drawing to create more realistic paintings** that captured nature's and humans' beauty better than ever before.

400. **Previously, art only centered on depicting religious figures and lacked character and storytelling.** During the Renaissance, it focused on the human body, harkening back to the classical Greek style.

401. **Famous artists from the Renaissance include Michelangelo, Leonardo da Vinci, and Raphael,** who created marvelous pieces of art and sculptures that still dazzle viewers to this day.

402. **The printing press was invented in Germany during the Renaissance by Johannes Gutenberg.** The printing press allowed books to be printed faster than handwritten manuscripts.

403. **The Renaissance saw the invention of new instruments, such as the violin and harpsichord,** which allowed more complex musical compositions to be created.

404. **Scientists like Galileo Galilei began using telescopes to study the stars in detail,** leading Galileo to discover four moons orbiting Jupiter.

405. **Exploration was encouraged by many countries. Christopher Columbus made his famous voyage** across the Atlantic Ocean in 1492.

406. **Education systems were updated, with universities teaching students about humanist values, arts, and sciences,** in addition to theology and mathematics.

407. **The Renaissance slowly spread from Italy to central, western, and northern Europe.** Different regions experienced the Renaissance at different times. It wasn't a singular movement throughout all of Europe.

408. **In Italy, powerful merchant families like the Medici were patrons of the arts.** They funded many projects in Florence and Rome.

409. The Catholic Church commissioned artists to create pieces for different papal residences and palaces. The church's most famous commission is likely Michelangelo's painting on the ceiling of the Sistine Chapel.

410. The Renaissance was full of famous writers, such as Niccolo Machiavelli and William Shakespeare.

411. Architecture changed, with builders creating structures using innovative techniques and displaying classical Greek and Roman influences, such as the use of symmetrical arches, domes, pillars, and columns.

412. People became interested in studying nature through observation rather than relying on superstition or religion, which eventually led people toward the modern scientific methods we use today.

413. Leonardo da Vinci studied human anatomy by dissecting animal and human bodies. Although he never finished his book on anatomy, his ideas helped scientists make discoveries about the human body.

414. The Renaissance saw the invention of new weapons, such as cannons and guns, which changed how wars were fought.

415. New trading routes opened up between Europe, Africa, and Asia, allowing for goods like spices to become more easily accessible in European markets.

The Reformation
(16th century)

The 16th century was a period of profound transformation across Europe, and the Reformation was at its center. In this section, we will explore twenty interesting facts about the Reformation.

416. **The Protestant Reformation was an important religious movement in Europe during the 16th century,** which resulted in the Catholic Church splintering.

417. **The Reformation started when Martin Luther, a German monk and professor of theology,** posted his Ninety-five Theses on October 31st, 1517. He sought to challenge the Catholic Church's corrupt practices.

418. **There had been other, relatively minor, reform movements in Europe prior to Luther led by figures like John Wycliffe in England and the Czech Jan Hus.**

419. **Luther initially wrote the Ninety-seven Theses, which had a more theological viewpoint.** This work is largely ignored since the Ninety-five Theses is the one that started a revolution.

420. **The Protestant Reformation spread across Germany and other parts of Europe** over the next few decades.

421. **The Reformation was led by Luther and other influential figures, including Ulrich Zwingli in Switzerland and John Calvin in France.**

422. **One of Luther's problems with the Catholic Church was that it had become increasingly powerful and rich.** The church used its influence as leverage over the ordinary Christians of Europe, most of whom believed everything the church told them.

423. **Luther was mainly concerned with the practice of indulgences. During the Middle Ages,** people could go to church and pay for the salvation of their sins.

424. **Luther wanted his followers to read and understand the scriptures in order to find true Christian values.** He didn't want people to listen to only what was preached by the Catholic Church.

425. **The reformers also recognized that many members of the Catholic clergy were becoming increasingly less versed in Christian doctrine and theology,** as well as in their mastery of Latin.

426. **Luther's doctrine of justification by faith alone was heavily influential.** This idea asserted that an individual's true faith justified them in the eyes of God.

427. In 1521, **Martin Luther was excommunicated from the Catholic Church.**

428. **Luther managed to spread his controversial ideas very quickly thanks to the newly invented printing press.**

429. During this period, **new translations of the Bible were made in multiple languages so that people could read it for themselves** and interpret passages differently from what was traditionally taught by the church.

430. **The Reformation brought about a period of religious wars in Europe between Catholics and Protestants,** resulting in thousands of deaths.

431. **Religious freedom and tolerance became more accepted as a result of the Reformation.** The people wanted the freedom to choose which religion to follow.

432. **In France, Spain, and Italy, the Catholic Church was still more dominant.**

433. **Most places in Germany, Scandinavia, the Low Countries, and England converted to different forms of Protestantism.**

434. **In England, King Henry VIII declared himself the head of the church,** which resulted in the nation adopting Anglicanism (a form of Protestantism).

435. **Other countries created their own national churches, such as Lutheranism or Presbyterianism,** depending on who ruled the region.

436. **The Reformation had a great impact on art. Artists began to create works that emphasized religious themes and stories,** often in stark contrast to traditional Catholic artwork, which focused more on saints or biblical characters.

437. **Music was greatly affected by the Reformation.** Composers created hymns with lyrics taken directly from the scripture so ordinary laypeople could sing along while worshiping God at home or in church services.

438. **The Catholic Church responded to Protestantism by trying to reform itself,** leading to what is known today as **the Counter-Reformation or Catholic Reformation.** This movement brought about new laws, institutional changes, and educational reforms.

439. Ideas that began with **Luther's writings soon found their way into politics.** Elite circles began talking about more expression of individual freedoms, something that would eventually lead to the rise of democracy.

440. From the late 16th century onward, **many military conflicts between states were motivated by differences in religion, with Protestant and Catholic nations** taking up arms against each other.

The Thirty Years' War
(1618–1648)

The Thirty Years' War was one of the longest and most destructive wars in European history. This chapter will explore this major conflict with twenty interesting facts about how it started, who fought in it, and how it was resolved.

441. **The Thirty Years' War was a major conflict between Catholic and Protestant countries in Europe.** It was the last major European conflict that began because of religion.

442. **It started when the king of Bohemia and the Holy Roman emperor, Ferdinand II, tried to impose Catholicism on all his subjects in 1618.**

443. **The Protestant nobles of the empire started a rebellion, which would be dealt with by Ferdinand.**

444. In 1625, **Denmark declared war on the Holy Roman Empire, hoping to support the German princes in their anti-Catholic cause.** Sweden declared war on the Holy Roman Empire in 1629.

445. **Emperor Ferdinand's decision was very controversial since the 1555 Peace of Augsburg had guaranteed German princes the right to practice either Catholicism or Protestantism.**

446. **The war would drag in other kingdoms like France, Spain, and Poland.** These nations allied with the German princes to exploit instability and weaken the Holy Roman Empire or joined the Holy Roman Empire to fight for Catholicism.

447. **At the war's height, it involved almost every major state in Europe, with England being the notable exception.**

448. **The war lasted for thirty years** (1618–1648), making it one of the longest wars in European history.

449. **It caused widespread destruction across Germany,** resulting in famine, disease, and huge population losses of up to 40 percent.

450. **The Peace of Westphalia ended this war by granting freedom of religion to central Europe,** allowing more people to practice their faith openly without persecution or interference from rulers.

451. **This treaty also started to put an end to feudalism in Europe** and allowed for the development of stronger nation-states.

452. **The Peace of Westphalia established international boundaries that largely remain intact today,** such as those between France, Germany, Austria, and Switzerland.

453. **The war was fought mainly on German soil,** but it had a major impact on other European countries.

454. **One of the most famous figures to rise from this conflict was King Gustavus Adolphus of Sweden,** who is regarded as one of history's greatest generals.

455. **The Thirty Years' War saw some early military innovations, such as the use of pike formations,** improved artillery tactics, and better siege warfare techniques.

456. **It began a period known as the age of absolute monarchies.** Rulers had more power over their citizens than ever before, allowing them to raise taxes and levy armies with little oversight from other governing bodies or the citizens themselves.

457. **This war saw the introduction of more professional armies,** which were paid by taxes instead of relying on volunteers or conscription.

458. **The war helped usher in an era known as the Enlightenment,** a period when philosophers began questioning old ideas about politics and society.

459. **The Thirty Years' War resulted in tens of thousands of casualties for all sides;** it is estimated that up to a million people died of warfare and disease during this time, making it the largest-scale war in European history up to that point.

460. **The Thirty Years' War is often considered to be the first major conflict in the history of Europe** that was fought by the great European powers.

The Age of Exploration
(15th–17th Centuries)

The Age of Exploration was a period marked by remarkable discoveries, advancements in sailing technology, and trade networks between different countries. This chapter will explore twenty-five interesting facts about this era. Get ready for an exciting voyage into the past!

461. **The Age of Exploration was a period from the 15th to the 17th century** when people explored new lands and oceans in search of trade, wealth, and knowledge.

462. **The fall of Constantinople in 1453 led European countries to scramble to find new routes to the East after the Ottomans closed their access to the Silk Road.**

463. **Many European countries competed against each other to claim land and establish colonies** in newly discovered territories.

464. **Many consider Christopher Columbus's voyage to be the start of the Age of Exploration.** However, he was not the first European to discover the Americas. Leif Erikson, a Viking, discovered North America about one thousand years before Columbus set sail.

465. **Portuguese explorer Vasco da Gama became the first person to sail directly from Europe to India,** reaching the subcontinent in 1498 by traveling down the African coast to India's western coast via the Indian Ocean route that he had uncovered during his explorations.

466. **An Italian navigator named Amerigo Vespucci provided evidence that Columbus did not discover Asia but had reached mainland America.**

467. **The Americas get their name from Amerigo Vespucci!**

468. **Ferdinand Magellan led a fleet of ships on an epic voyage that circumnavigated the world in 1522.** His crew became the first to travel around the world by ship.

469. **Magellan would not survive the voyage, dying in the Philippines.**

470. **Hernán Cortés was a Spanish conquistador who conquered Mexico for Spain** in 1521 after defeating Aztec leader Montezuma II.

471. **Francisco Pizarro conquered Peru from the Incas in 1533** with just a few hundred men at his disposal.

472. **The European powers had a huge advantage compared to the natives thanks to their advanced military technology.** They had guns and cannons at their disposal and wore heavy armor. The natives fought back with bows and spears.

473. **The natives were also decimated by European diseases,** which reduced the number of people who could fight for the land.

474. **Some of the major diseases that were spread were smallpox, measles, and influenza.** It is believed up to 95 percent of natives living in the Americas died of disease or from conflicts.

475. **European powers, such as Portugal, Spain, England, and France, explored new lands for resources like gold and spices,** which could be sold at high prices, making these countries wealthier.

476. **The Portuguese established trading posts or fortresses throughout Africa, India, and China,** allowing them access to valuable resources.

477. **Spain emerged as the most dominant overseas empire during the early days of the Age of Exploration.**

478. **Spanish possessions included much of North, Central, and South America, in addition to the Philippines.**

479. **France, Great Britain, and eventually the Netherlands would emerge as dominant European colonizers,** following in the footsteps of the Portuguese and Spanish.

480. **Jesuit missionaries traveled to these new lands, spreading Christianity to the places they visited.**

481. **In North America, British migrants established small colonies centered** around their Protestant denominations.

482. **Globalization began because of these explorations since it allowed for the spread of new ideas,** products, technology, and religion.

483. **Maps were made with greater accuracy thanks to the data collected by navigators during their voyages.**

484. **African slaves were captured and then transported across the Atlantic or Indian Ocean,** where they would be sold as slaves and used as laborers or domestic workers in European colonies.

485. **The Age of Exploration brought remarkable advances in sailing technology,** such as better ship designs and navigation tools like the astrolabe.

The Scientific Revolution
(17th century)

The Scientific Revolution of the 17th century brought about immense changes in scientific understanding and discovery. These twenty interesting facts will shed light on the major discoveries that were made, as well as some of the influential scientists of this period.

486. **The Scientific Revolution refers to a period in European history that took mostly during the 16th and 17th centuries** when a new view of science and scientific thought became prominent, one that was free from philosophy and religion and was based on the scientific method.

487. **Scientists like Galileo, Johannes Kepler, and Isaac Newton** made huge advances in understanding the world around them. They used observation and experimentation instead of relying on ancient texts or superstitions.

488. **In 1610, Galileo used his telescope to observe four moons orbiting Jupiter;** he named them after figures from Greek mythology.

489. **Johannes Kepler discovered three laws of motion that helped explain why planets move in an elliptical shape around the sun** as opposed to in perfect circles, which had been believed since antiquity.

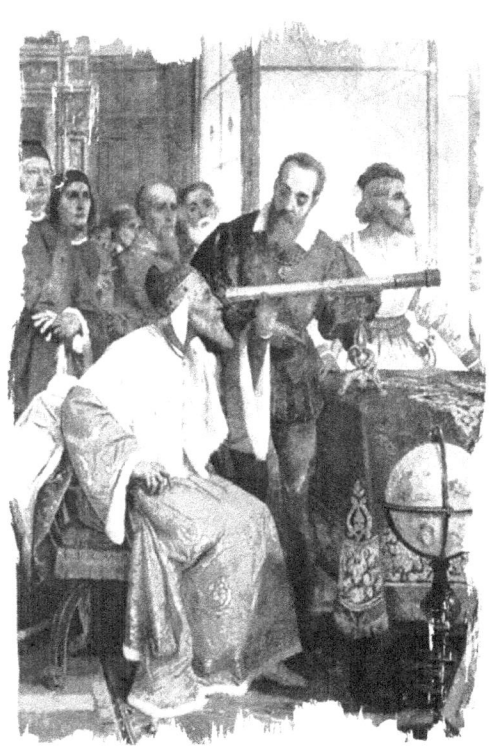

490. **Isaac Newton developed calculus, which allowed for more accurate calculations when studying movement,** such as gravity, along with forces acting upon objects.

491. **Newton developed his famous law of universal gravitation,** stating all objects attract each other through gravitational force depending on their mass.

492. **New ideas were spread across Europe due to developments in printing technology,** which allowed scientists' work to be published for wider audiences.

493. **By the end of the Scientific Revolution,** scientists had begun to use hypotheses and theories as tools to gain a deeper understanding of nature.

494. In the 1600s, **William Harvey discovered how blood circulates in human bodies by experimenting with animals like dogs and chickens.**

495. **Robert Boyle developed a law called Boyle's Law,** which states that pressure and volume are related when it comes to gases. This later became known as one of the most important laws of physics!

496. **Antonie Van Leeuwenhoek used the microscope he invented to observe bacteria,** red blood cells, spermatozoa, capillaries, and other small organisms for the first time.

497. **Antoine Lavoisier is considered the father of modern chemistry** due to his development of chemical nomenclature (names) and methods like oxidation, which changed how people studied matter.

498. **William Gilbert studied magnetism and electricity in depth.** He wrote a book on the subject called De Magnete, which helped others understand how these forces worked together.

499. **Francis Bacon developed an approach to scientific research known as empiricism,** which involves using observation and experimentation rather than relying solely on ancient texts or superstition to find answers about natural phenomena.

500. **Blaise Pascal made major contributions to mathematics and physics,** being one of the most avid defenders of the scientific method.

501. **René Descartes is most famous for developing the idea of "cogito ergo sum,"** or "I think, therefore I am," though he also made significant contributions to the field of mathematics through his development of Cartesian or analytic geometry.

502. **Ole Roemer developed a new way of measuring longitude,** which helped improve navigation on ships. He also studied light speed and made calculations about Earth's motion around the sun.

503. **Institutions such as the French Academy of Sciences in Paris and the Royal Society of London** for Improving Natural Knowledge helped accelerate scientific research and make the knowledge available to the masses.

504. **All of these new discoveries questioned the strength and legitimacy of old institutions,** most notably the church.

505. **Although women made some important contributions, they were not allowed to join the prestigious societies.** One important female thinker from this time was Maria Sibylla Merian, whose research on insects led to the discovery of life cycles.

The Age of Enlightenment
(18th century)

The Age of Enlightenment was a period where many people rejected traditional authority and embraced knowledge obtained through science and reason. This chapter will explore twenty facts about the impact that the Age of Enlightenment had on society.

506. **The Age of Enlightenment lasted from the late 17th century to the early 19th century.** It was a time when many people questioned authority and tradition, believing knowledge should be gained through reason and science instead.

507. **It started in Europe but spread around the world to places such as North America and South America.**

508. During this era, **new ideas about government, religion, science, and philosophy emerged.**

509. **Rene Descartes is often regarded as an important thinker who helped kickstart the Age of Enlightenment with his Discourse on the Method (1637).**

510. **Famous figures from this period include Voltaire, Jean-Jacques Rousseau, Benjamin Franklin, and Thomas Jefferson.** These thinkers helped shape modern society with their writings and philosophies on life.

511. **Newspapers were widely circulated during the Age of Enlightenment,** which allowed for discussions between citizens and led to changes in how governments were run across Europe.

512. **Many Enlightenment thinkers believed in religious tolerance and the freedom of speech,** seeing them as natural human rights.

513. **A lot of art was created that symbolized new values related to human rights, such as liberty or patriotism.** These included paintings like Jacques Louis David's Death of Marat (1793) and Francisco Goya's Third of May (1808).

514. **New ideas about education were developed that emphasized the importance of individual learning and critical thinking skills** over memorization or rote learning.

515. **The Age of Enlightenment had a major influence on the American Revolution, the French Revolution,** and other political upheavals in Europe during and after this period.

516. **Many countries tried to adopt constitutional governments to replace monarchies, although it would take time for this to happen.** The people began to believe more in a democracy than absolute power.

517. **The United States of America broke away from Great Britain.** It declared independence from colonial rule and set up its own set of laws based on principles from Enlightenment philosophy.

518. **This era saw an increase in literacy.** Books became easier to access due to cheaper printing methods.

519. **The use of reason was seen as key, with many philosophers believing in the power of logical thinking and debate** to answer questions about life and society.

520. **The importance of reason and rational thinking were some of the values that had largely been lost after the fall of the Roman Empire.**

521. **Human rights started to be discussed more seriously during this period,** leading to reforms such as abolishing the slave trade in some parts of Europe, though not all.

522. **Coffee houses were popular among intellectuals,** who would gather there to discuss ideas on politics, science, and other topics while enjoying their drinks.

523. **The colony of Australia was established in 1788. Prisoners from Britain** were sent there instead of being held prisoner in their home country.

524. **This period saw an increase in public education,** which allowed more people to have access to knowledge and learning opportunities.

525. **One important philosopher was John Locke.** He believed the mind was a tabula rasa (blank slate) at birth and that knowledge came from experience.

The Industrial Revolution
(18th–19th Centuries)

The Industrial Revolution marked a major turning point in human history. This section will take a closer look at this period by exploring twenty interesting facts about how people worked and lived, as well as some of the technological innovations that were discovered.

526. **The Industrial Revolution began in Britain in the late 1700s.** It was a period of new inventions and technology that made machines more powerful and faster than ever before.

527. **During the Industrial Revolution, factories were built to produce goods faster and cheaper than before.** This allowed people to buy things they previously could not afford.

528. **Coal and steam power were used to run these factories.**

529. **Thousands of jobs were created.** Many people moved from farms to cities, looking for new opportunities.

530. **Textiles like cotton and wool became big industries during this time.** Factory-made cloth replaced handspun clothing produced at home or on small looms.

531. **Innovations like the cotton gin allowed farmers to produce larger quantities of cotton much faster than before.** This drove down prices, which made clothing more widely accessible to all social classes.

532. **Railroads became an important means of transportation for both raw materials needed in industrial production processes and finished products.**

533. **New sources of energy, such as petroleum fuel oil,** enabled ships to carry goods around the world much more quickly.

534. **The development of a technique called the Bessemer process made it possible to mass-produce steel,** which was used in many new inventions and machines during this era.

535. **The telegraph changed how people communicated with one another.** This invention was followed by the invention of the telephone by Alexander Graham Bell.

536. **The Industrial Revolution saw an increase in life expectancy,** as advances in medicine increased access to better healthcare for more people.

537. **Many women found new work opportunities in factories or mills.** There was a lot of gender inequality at this time, and becoming a major part of the workforce led to suffrage movements.

538. **Immigration rates rose significantly during this period,** with millions of Europeans traveling in search of new jobs and lives. Many Europeans moved to the United States.

539. **The Industrial Revolution changed the way people shopped.** Stores began to offer a greater variety of goods and extended credit options for customers who could not afford upfront payments.

540. **Machine tools were created that allowed for faster production times with fewer workers needed,** resulting in lower labor costs that made many products affordable to more people.

541. **Production processes became standardized, leading to improved quality control for mass-produced goods.** Consumers knew what they were buying was reliable.

542. **Gas lighting replaced candles or lamps,** providing safer light sources in homes since there wasn't a risk of fire from open flames.

543. **Industrialization came with a lot of drawbacks.** For example, Europe saw an increase in pollution due to the burning of coal, oil, and other materials used for power generation.

544. **Factory workers often had to work long hours under dangerous conditions.** They received very little pay, and there were few protections in place.

545. In 1712, **James Watt invented the steam engine.** Steam power became the most popular energy source for machines and transportation.

The French Revolution
(1789–1799)

The French Revolution was one of the most tumultuous and influential periods in European history. In this chapter, we will explore thirty interesting facts about the revolution, including how it began, its significant leaders, and its impactful reforms.

546. **The French Revolution saw France change from an absolute monarchy to a republic with democratic ideals.**

547. **It began in 1787, and it would last until 1799, when Napoleon Bonaparte emerged on the scene to take control of France.**

548. **The general reasons behind the revolution included high taxes and prices,** poverty, a national economic crisis, and the struggling state of the peasant population of France.

549. **King Louis XVI was a very unpopular figure.** He lived an extremely lavish life, as did the members of the upper echelons of society, something that fueled dissent against the commoners.

550. **The revolution began when an institution called the Estates-General was summoned by the French finance minister** to deal with the economic crisis.

551. **The Estates-General was composed of the First Estate** (the clergy), **the Second Estate** (nobility), and **the Third Estate** (the commoners).

552. **The Third Estate was the largest, containing six hundred members**, while the First and Second Estates contained three hundred members each. However, each estate only got one vote each.

553. **The Third Estate wanted more power since they were the biggest group.** It declared itself a new body, the National Assembly, which threatened to proceed without the consent of the other estates.

554. **The National Assembly swore an oath not to disband before it had given France a new constitution** and forced the other members of the Estates-General to join it.

555. On July 14th, 1789, **thousands of enraged people in Paris stormed the Bastille, which was a prison fortress.** They were looking for gunpowder and weapons.

556. **The French saw the Bastille as a symbol for the monarchy's tyranny.** Bastille Day is still celebrated to this day!

557. **After storming the Bastille, revolutionaries formed their own armed force called the National Guard,** with the intention of putting up better resistance against those loyal to the throne.

558. **Popular French writers, like Voltaire, wrote satirical stories** poking fun at government officials, which helped fuel public discontentment before and during the revolution.

559. **King Louis XVI tried to flee Paris with his family to organize a counter-revolution in June of 1791,** but was arrested at the small town of Varennes northeast of the French capital.

560. **The new regime led by the National Constituent Assembly introduced a range of reforms that weakened the nobility and the church.** It redistributed lands to pay off public debt, gave new rights to lower classes, and implemented a new administrative system to better govern the country.

561. **The Declaration of the Rights of Man and of the Citizen asserted the universal values of liberty, equality, and brotherhood were essential values.**

562. **Queen Marie Antoinette, the wife of Louis XVI, was a strong opponent of the revolution.** She was also arrested after the royal family tried to flee France.

563. **Marie Antoinette is well known for saying, "Let them eat cake,"** but there is no evidence to suggest that she ever said these words.

564. **In 1792, France was dragged into a war with European powers that wished to put an end to the revolution** since it threatened the positions of absolute monarchs throughout the continent.

565. **The war ended with a French defeat,** but the monarchy was not reinstated by the foreign powers.

566. **The revolution saw many different political factions, such as the Girondins, the Montagnards, and the Jacobins,** who fought for their own versions of what the new France should look like.

567. **In 1793, both King Louis XVI and Queen Marie Antoinette were tried and executed.** They were charged with high treason.

568. **Maximilien Robespierre rose to prominence during the French Revolution.** He took harsh measures against those suspected to be against the revolution.

569. **Robespierre led his own political party called the Jacobins. They wanted equality before the law,** but they also believed strongly in executing anyone who opposed their cause.

570. **The Reign of Terror was a violent period during which hundreds of thousands of people were arrested.** Thousands died by guillotine in an effort to "purify" France. Robespierre himself was beheaded on July 28th, 1794.

571. In 1795, **a new government was formed called the Directory.** It was composed of five members that co-governed the state.

572. **After the formation of the Directory, a young general named Napoleon Bonaparte** started to rise in prominence for his military victories during a military campaign in Italy.

573. **France experienced massive cultural changes during the revolution.** It adopted a new national anthem, adopted the metric system, established public education for all citizens (including girls), and abolished slavery in its colonies.

574. **Napoleon would gain a lot of popularity and support from his own troops.** He and some followers overthrew the Directory in 1799 in the Coup of the 18 Brumaire.

575. **The coup abolished the Directory and established the new three-person Consulate, with Napoleon at its head,** leading to a new era in European history.

The Napoleonic Wars
(1803–1815)

The Napoleonic Wars were a series of battles fought between many countries in Europe. This section will explore thirty facts about this period, including the countries involved and how the conflicts impacted Europe.

576. **The Napoleonic Wars refers to a series of military campaigns fought between 1803 and 1815.** These conflicts were between France and other European states, most notably Great Britain, Austria, Russia, Prussia, Portugal, Spain, and Sweden.

577. After becoming First Consul with the Coup of 18 Brumaire, **Napoleon assumed almost total control of revolutionary France in 1799.**

578. **Upon gaining power, Napoleon implemented a range of political and economic reforms** that strengthened his position and helped France recover from the terrible events it had suffered during the French Revolution.

579. **Napoleon reorganized the French Army, introducing new recruitment and conscription laws and making it much stronger than it had been before.** He also chose to lead the army personally.

580. In 1803, **Great Britain declared war on France,** having noticed France's recent rise in power and Napoleon's declared interest in spreading the ideals of the French Revolution to the rest of Europe.

581. In October 1805, **French naval forces were crushed by the British at the Battle of Trafalgar.** This battle is well known for **the death of Horatio Nelson**, who became a British legend.

582. **Napoleon achieved a great victory against a combined Austro-Russian army at the Battle of Austerlitz** in late 1805. This battle led to the creation of **the Confederation of the Rhine,** which eventually led to the end of **the Holy Roman Empire.**

583. **The British Royal Navy was one of the most powerful navies in the world** at the time. It kept Napoleon from launching an invasion of Britain.

584. **Napoleon defeated the Austrian, Prussian, German, Swedish, and Russian coalitions** until he gained control over most of western and central Europe by 1809.

585. In 1807, **Napoleon led an invasion into Portugal, Britain's ally, and occupied Lisbon.**

586. **Napoleon deposed the Spanish king and installed his brother as the new king of Spain in 1808.**

587. **There was a widespread revolt in Iberia, where a large portion of Napoleon's forces were occupied for six years,** having to fight fierce opposition from Spanish and Portuguese guerilla fighters before their eventual defeat in 1814.

588. **Napoleon organized a blockade called the Continental System against Britain,** which limited the European states' ability to trade with the British. Napoleon wanted to weaken his rival economically.

589. In 1812, **Russia supposedly broke its pledge as a member of the Continental System. Napoleon decided to invade Russia** with an army of over 600,000 soldiers because of this and other reasons.

590. **The invasion of Russia would become his greatest mistake. The Russians never met the French in battle,** drawing them into the remote Russian heartland and razing towns and villages during their retreat.

591. **In Russia, Napoleon's army suffered terrible casualties due to the extreme cold and Russian tactics.** Only about 10 percent of Napoleon's soldiers survived the campaign.

592. **France never recovered from the Russian campaign.** Its rivals consolidated their forces once again and defeated Napoleon at Leipzig in 1813.

593. **Coalition forces, consisting of Austria, Prussia, and Russia,** captured Paris in March 1814.

594. **Napoleon was forced to abdicate. He was exiled to Elba,** an island in the Mediterranean Sea off the coast of Italy.

595. In 1815, **Napoleon escaped from exile but was finally defeated at the Battle of Waterloo by a British-led coalition led by Duke Wellington.**

596. **Some believe Napoleon could have won the battle. The heavy rains that took place made Napoleon delay his plans,** which gave the coalition time to regroup.

597. **The Battle of Waterloo is considered one of the most famous battles in European history.** It was the second-bloodiest battle that took place during the Napoleonic Wars.

598. **The Congress of Vienna (1814–1815) resulted in the formation of a new political order in Europe,** which became known as the Concert of Europe. It was meant to maintain the balance of power in the continent.

599. **The wars changed military tactics permanently.** For example, guerrilla warfare became more popular due to its effectiveness against larger armies.

600. **It is believed millions of civilians died due to war-related diseases or famine.**

601. **Many technological advancements occurred during this period.** For example, new types of muskets and artillery were developed, which allowed armies to fire more rapidly than ever before.

602. **Napoleon's efforts to spread a unified system of laws across Europe, known as the Napoleonic Code,** were crucial for individual states in establishing their own system of laws.

603. **During these wars, there was an upsurge in nationalism among European populations** that eventually led to the formation of modern nation-states, such as Italy and Germany.

604. **Napoleon's decline meant the rise of Britain.** The British consolidated their economic power and possessed the most powerful navy in the world.

605. **France lost all of the territories it gained during the wars.** Russia added much of Poland to its control, and Prussia gained lands as well.

The Greek War of Independence
(1821–1829)

The Greek War of Independence was a major event in modern history that saw Greece fight for its independence. This chapter will explore this fascinating period and look at twenty-five interesting facts about it.

606. **The Greek War of Independence was fought from 1821 to 1829.** Greek nationalists wanted to gain **independence from the Ottoman Empire** and establish a sovereign Greek state.

607. **This war was a very influential conflict that established many international precedents** and helped shape the way for future revolutionary wars against empires.

608. **A group called the Filiki Eteria** ("Society of Friends") was an important part of beginning **the revolution against the Ottomans,** who had ruled over Greece since 1453 CE.

609. **The Filiki Eteria was inspired by the French Revolution,** whose events had made it clear that people belonging to the same nation could come together to overthrow absolute rule.

610. **This group included prominent figures like Alexander Ypsilantis, Theodoros Kolokotronis, Demetrius Ypsilantis, and Georgios Karaiskakis.**

611. **The leader of the Greek Revolution was a man named Ioannis Kapodistrias,** who later became the first prime minister of Greece after independence had been achieved. He was called the governor of Greece.

612. **The revolution was planned to begin on March 25th, 1821, but the conspirators were forced to start the insurrection a month earlier since the Ottomans found out about their plans.**

613. **In February 1821, Greeks in the Peloponnese region rose up against their Ottoman rulers** and declared independence for Greece.

614. **Famous intellectuals believed so strongly in the Greeks' cause.** American physician Samuel Howe and English poet Lord Byron joined the revolution.

615. **The first flag of independent Greece was based on an ancient symbol known as the cross-in-square, which is still used today by many Orthodox churches around the world.**

616. **Many countries, such as Britain and France, supported Greece during this war,** but Russia became its most powerful ally.

617. **These European powers sent their fleets to provide much-needed naval assistance to Greek revolutionaries** who were being outmatched at sea by the Ottomans.

618. **The Ottoman Empire had experienced a long period of decline,** which allowed many different nationalities under its control to challenge it and fight for independence.

619. **Greek revolts sparked up all around the Ottoman Empire.** The Ottomans were unable to deal with all of them and were forced to reorganize their defenses.

620. **The Ottoman forces were so badly organized that they suffered heavy defeats** at the hands of the Greek military forces, even at sea.

621. **The Ottomans requested aid from Egypt to counter the Greek victories,** but international pressure rendered their efforts useless.

622. **The Battle of Navarino in 1827 was a major victory for the Greeks and helped them gain international recognition from countries like Britain, Russia, and France.**

623. **At an assembly known as the London Protocol, Great Britain and Russia jointly recognized an independent Greece in 1830,** something that was reaffirmed two years later when the Ottoman Empire accepted its defeat.

624. **Prince Otto von Wittelsbach from Bavaria was chosen by King George IV of England to become Greece's first monarch.** He did not have much success due to political unrest in Greece, which lasted until 1862, when he was deposed.

625. **Greece's national anthem is called "Hymn to Liberty,"** which was written by Dionysios Solomos in 1823.

626. **After gaining independence, Greece was made into a constitutional monarchy.** The monarchy was abolished in the late 20th century.

627. **The war saw significant advances in naval technology, such as the development of steam-powered ships,** something that helped to ensure victory at battles such as Navarino.

628. **Interestingly, Haiti, which had gained its independence from France a couple of decades earlier,** was the first nation to recognize Greece as a fully sovereign nation.

629. **The Treaty of Constantinople,** signed in 1832, defined the new borders between Greece and the Ottoman Empire.

630. **The Greek War of Independence led to other countries, such as Serbia, Bulgaria, and Romania, g**aining their independence from Ottoman rule.

The Crimean War
(1853–1856)

The Crimean War was a major international conflict that involved millions of soldiers. In this chapter, we explore twenty fascinating facts about this war, including the technologies that were used, a nurse's heroic efforts, and more!

631. **The Crimean War was fought between Russia and an alliance of countries, including Britain, France, and the Ottoman Empire.**

632. **It lasted from 1853 to 1856 and involved millions of soldiers on both sides.** They fought various battles across Europe and the Middle East.

633. **It began when Russian troops invaded the Ottoman Empire's territory of Crimea** after a disagreement about who should control it.

634. **One of the reasons behind the outbreak of the war was the alleged mistreatment of Eastern Orthodox subjects in Ottoman-controlled Palestine.**

635. **Russia demanded that the Eastern Orthodox population of the Ottoman Empire be placed under the protection of Tsar Nicholas I,** something that was rejected by the Ottoman government as it would have given Russia considerable influence.

636. **It was after this refusal that Russia decided to launch an invasion of Ottoman lands in July of 1853,** attacking Ottoman-controlled Romania.

637. **Another reason behind Russia's aggressive policy was the declining strength of the Ottoman Empire,** which put the future of Europe's balance of power established after the Napoleonic Wars into question.

638. **The allied forces won two key naval victories over Russian fleets at Sinope** (in modern-day Turkey) in November 1853 and Taganrog Bay (in modern-day Russia) in January 1855.

639. **The siege of Sevastopol, which lasted for eleven months, was the decisive turning point for the war.** The allied forces managed to defeat the Russians after very intense fighting.

640. **Russia sued for peace after the defeat at Sevastopol,** fearing that its heartland would be invaded by the allied forces.

641. **The conflict ended with a victory for Britain, France,** and the Ottoman Empire. Russia had to give up some of its lands near Crimea with **the Treaty of Paris of 1856.**

642. **The British and French supported the Ottomans because they feared the empire would have been decisively defeated by the Russians,** which would upset the balance of power in Europe.

643. **Diseases like cholera and typhus killed more soldiers during the Crimean War than fighting did.**

644. **The war saw one of the first uses of photography to document battles and conditions on battlefields as battles unfolded,** helping people back home understand what was happening in real time.

645. **The Crimean War is sometimes referred to as the first "modern" war.**

646. **Lord Aberdeen, the prime minister of the United Kingdom, resigned soon after the Treaty of Paris was signed.** The public was upset about the mismanagement and high cost of the war.

647. **Many paintings depicting scenes from the Crimean War became popular across Europe,** such as William Simpson's painting Charge of the Heavy Brigade at Balaklava.

648. **Florence Nightingale, a famous English nurse, set up field hospitals and trained nurses at Scutari Hospital near Istanbul,** where she treated wounded soldiers and used improved sanitation practices.

649. **The Crimean War greatly weakened the Russian army.** It would take decades for Russia to recover.

650. **Leo Tolstoy, the famous Russian author who wrote War and Peace, served during the Crimean War.**

The Revolutions of 1848

This chapter will explore the fascinating history of the revolutions of 1848 by taking a look at twenty interesting facts about this period. Why did they start? Were any reforms made because of them? Through these facts, we'll be able to gain an understanding of why this period was so significant for many European countries!

651. **The revolutions of 1848 were a series of uprisings that happened in many countries in Europe** in the mid-19th century.

652. **This period is often called the Springtime of Nations due to its widespread nature,** prominence of nationalist sentiments, and hope for positive outcomes.

653. **The revolutions began in France, where people demanded more freedom and democracy from the government.**

654. **During the June Days, barricades were built by protestors on the streets of Paris.** They were protesting proposed reforms by the government.

655. **The French police brutally suppressed the protesters,** resulting in about ten thousand casualties and thousands of deportations.

656. **Inspired by the events in France, people across Europe protested against their rulers** to gain more rights and be represented more fairly in government.

657. **The revolutions spread quickly to other countries, including Austria, Prussia (now Germany), Italy, and Hungary.**

658. **In Vienna, there was an uprising called the March Revolution,** with university students leading a march through the city and demanding reform.

659. **The revolutions of 1848 were a turning point for Europe,** as it was the first time popular movements had come together to fight for change in multiple countries.

660. **The results of the revolutions varied from place to place, but on the whole,** the intended outcomes of establishing liberal governments or nation-states were unsuccessful.

661. In some places, **like France, protests led to the adoption of a new constitution,** which guaranteed some new rights.

662. **The small German states demanded German unification. While this was not achieved in 1848,** it fueled sentiment that would last until German unification in 1871.

663. **Italy saw some reforms, including abolishing censorship of books and newspapers,** which helped spread more information among citizens.

664. **In the Austrian Empire, which contained people from many different nations,** the revolution posed a great threat to Habsburg rule.

665. **With the help of Russian military intervention, the Habsburgs were able to brutally suppress the revolutionaries.** The revolutionaries achieved limited progress toward liberalism.

666. **Hungary declared itself independent from Austrian rule. Lajos Kossuth became its leader** and introduced many reforms, such as abolishing feudalism and granting land to the peasantry.

667. **The revolutions of 1848 sparked a wave of migration from Europe to North America,** leading to one of the largest migrant waves in American history.

668. **Writers like Victor Hugo wrote about these revolutions at the time,** which helped spread awareness among citizens.

669. **Karl Marx and Friedrich Engels famously wrote The Communist Manifesto in 1848, outlining their vision for a communist society.** Marx was involved in the German revolution of 1848.

670. **Although many of the revolutions during the Springtime of Nations would fail to achieve their intended outcomes, they would spark a broader sense of liberal nationalism throughout the continent.** The revolutions led to very influential developments, such as the formation of countries as we know them today.

The Unification of Germany
(1871)

This chapter will explore the historic unification of Germany in 1871. We'll take a look at twenty-five interesting facts about how separate German-speaking states joined together to form one country and the role played by Otto von Bismarck.

671. **The unification of Germany happened in 1871 when German-speaking states joined to form one country called Germany.**

672. **Ever since the dawn of the Holy Roman Empire,** the territory of modern-day Germany was divided between hundreds of smaller states, baronies, duchies, and city-states.

673. **These political entities, for the most part, all shared a common German culture and language,** but the complex political dynamics and structures within the Holy Roman Empire had made it nearly impossible to form a united German state.

674. **This changed after the Napoleonic Wars.** Napoleon defeated and reorganized the German states, abolishing the Holy Roman Empire.

675. **By the time of Germany's unification in 1871, there were still up to forty independent German states, with the Kingdom of Prussia,** located in the north, being the largest.

676. **In almost all of the German states, revolutionary and nationalist sentiments were expressed during the Springtime of Nations,** so the spirit for unification was high by the time the process began.

677. **The unification process was led by Prussian Chancellor Otto von Bismarck,** an excellent diplomat who realized that the possibility of German unification under Prussia was possible.

678. **A major opponent of Bismarck and Prussia was the Habsburg Austrian Empire, which also spoke German and shared the German culture.** The Austrian Empire had economic and political interests in unifying the smaller German states.

679. In 1834, **the German states were united in an economic union, the Zollverein, which was led by Prussia.**

680. **At the beginning of the 1860s, Bismarck realized that Austria had been weakened by its recent defeat in a war against France and the Kingdom of Piedmont.** He knew that it was time to start the process of unification.

681. **Otto von Bismarck famously declared in a speech in 1862,** "The great questions of the time will not be resolved by speeches and majority decisions … but by iron and blood." This statement reflected his belief in the importance of military power in achieving German unity.

682. **In 1866, Prussia and Austria went to war over a German province on the border with Denmark named Holstein. Austria' was defeated in just over six weeks.**

683. **The first official leader of a united Germany was Kaiser Wilhelm I,** who came from Prussia's royal family, the Hohenzollern dynasty.

684. **In 1866, Prussia proclaimed the creation of the North German Confederation,** which it would lead.

685. **The North German Confederation adopted the North German Constitution,** which made it a constitutional monarchy based on federalism.

686. From 1866 to 1871, **Bismarck initiated domestic policies that served to strengthen local production and stimulate economic growth.** He also retrained the military.

687. **In 1870, Prussia, with the support of the North German Confederation,** went to war with France. France was seen as the new main rival after Austria's defeat.

688. **The Franco-Prussian War of 1870–1871 played a crucial role in the unification of Germany,** with the Prussians able to achieve a decisive victory that had been largely unexpected.

689. **At the Palace of Versailles, the German Empire, or the German Reich, was officially proclaimed on January 18th, 1871,** with Kaiser Wilhelm I becoming its first emperor.

690. **Prussia's victory over France weakened French influence in Europe and helped to rally support for German nationalism** and accelerate the process of unification.

691. **After reunification, Berlin became the capital city of Germany. It still is today.**

692. **A strong sense of nationalism has been associated with Germany,** and its citizens are proud to call themselves Germans regardless of their regional origin or background.

693. **German unification inspired many similar movements in Europe,** most notably the unification of Italy, which took place around the same time.

694. **The unification of Germany and its strong military created a new European superpower.** Germany became one of the most dominant nations in the continent.

695. **Thanks to Bismarck's talents as a diplomat, the German Empire experienced marvelous economic growth** that was directed to maintaining a professional army and the new balance of power in Europe.

The Unification of Italy (1871)

This chapter explores the Italian unification, a movement that saw many states unified into one country. We'll take a look at twenty-five interesting facts about how this was achieved, from key figures to revolts.

696. **The unification of Italy would conclude in 1871,** although the Italians' journey for unification began way back in 1848.

697. Much like Germany, **the Italian Peninsula in the 19th century was made up of smaller states** that largely shared a common culture.

698. **With the spread of liberal and nationalist ideas in the 19th century,** the Risorgimento movement was formed, which sought to unify the Italian nation.

699. **By the time the unification process began in the 1840s, the south of Italy was controlled by the Kingdom of the Two Sicilies,** the central territories were controlled by the Papal States, and the north of the peninsula was contested by several states, including **the Kingdom of Sardinia-Piedmont, the Duchy of Tuscany, and the Austrian-controlled Kingdom of Lombardy-Venetia.**

700. **The Carbonari group was crucial in Italian unification.** It had been created as a secret political organization in the early 19th century and pushed for Italian nationalism and independence from French and Habsburg influence.

701. **Two of the Carbonari leaders were Giuseppe Mazzini and Giuseppe Garibaldi.** They played important roles in Italian unification.

702. **Garibaldi was from Piedmont and escaped prison in 1834. He went to South America,** where he gained a lot of practice participating in Latin American revolutionary wars. He mastered the art of guerilla warfare and would return to Italy in 1848.

703. **Mazzini was the statesman of the Carbonari.** He was arrested a couple of times for revolutionary activities.

704. **The Kingdom of Sardinia-Piedmont would lead the process of Italian unification.**

705. In 1848, **during the First Italian War of Independence, the Kingdom of Sardinia-Piedmont went to war with Habsburg Austria.**

706. **Piedmont had the help of local revolutionaries.** They wanted to end conservative rule in Italian provinces controlled by Austria.

707. During the same year, there would be a liberal revolt against the Bourbon monarchy in the Kingdom of the Two Sicilies, which would be suppressed by the king.

708. **The First Italian War of Independence ended in an Austrian victory.** France intervened to restore the status quo and keep Italy disintegrated.

709. **Prime Minister Camillo Cavour eventually created an alliance between Sardinia-Piedmont and France against Habsburg Austria.** The two sides would go to war in 1859 during the Second War of Italian Independence.

710. **This time, the French and the Sardinians emerged victorious,** forcing Austria to cede control of the provinces of Lombardy, Modena, and Emilia.

711. **One year later, Giuseppe Garibaldi led a secret military expedition to overthrow the Sicilian monarchy and annex southern Italian provinces to the Kingdom of Sardinia-Piedmont.**

712. **The Expedition of the Thousand managed to liberate Sicily and overthrow the Sicilian monarchy.** The revolutionaries also took most of the Papal States' territories in central Italy.

713. In 1861, **the Kingdom of the Two Sicilies was annexed by united Italy following a referendum that saw 97 percent of Sicilians vote for unifying with Italy.**

714. **The united Kingdom of Italy was officially proclaimed in March 1861,** with the title of king assumed by Victor Emmanuel II of Sardinia.

715. **In 1866, the Kingdom of Italy, which controlled most of the Italian Peninsula, joined Prussia in defeating Austria.**

716. During the war, **the Kingdom of Italy claimed the Austrian Italian territories of Veneto, Friuli, and Mantua.**

717. **The unification of Italy would be completed in 1871 with the annexation of Rome after a German victory in the Franco-Prussian War.**

718. **Pope Pius IX opposed unification, something that led to the Papal States being annexed by Italy following the capture of Rome in 1870, ending papal rule in Italy.**

719. **Rome became the capital city after it was incorporated into Italy.**

720. **After unification took place, there were more investments in infrastructure,** which led to improvements in industrialization, railway networks, and education systems.

721. **Unification helped shape modern Italy and its culture as we know it today,** including music, art, and literature.

722. **Italian unification was a long and difficult process that took many decades to complete, unlike German unification,** which was achieved in the span of about fifteen years.

723. **Prime Minister Camillo Cavour passed away shortly after unification had taken place.** His efforts are still remembered today for helping to create modern-day Italy.

724. **The national anthem of Italy, "Il Canto degli Italiani," was composed in 1847** during the height of nationalist sentiment. It is the country's national anthem today.

725. **The design for the modern national flag of Italy was adopted during Italy's unification.** The tricolor flag was used by **Sardinian Carbonari** and later spread all around the nation.

The Scramble for Africa and Bismarck's Europe
(1871–1914)

The Scramble for Africa, which took place primarily during the late 19th and early 20th centuries, was a period of intense colonization and imperial expansion by European powers across **the African continent.** This era also saw **the rise of Prussia.** These thirty interesting facts will shed light on this formative period in European history.

726. **The last three decades of the 19th century and the first decade of the 20th century** saw a series of political maneuvers in Europe that culminated with the outbreak of World War I.

727. **With the unification of Italy and Germany, two new powerful empires had been created in Europe.** They were in competition with the already strong French, British, Russian, and Austrian superpowers.

728. **To maintain the balance of power between these large empires and prevent the outbreak of a major conflict, Otto von Bismarck** believed it was necessary to contain France, which had run over all of **Europe during Napoleon's reign.**

729. **In 1879, Germany entered a defensive alliance with Austria-Hungary. Italy joined in 1882, making it the Triple Alliance.**

730. **All three states agreed to secret arrangements and pledged to follow each other in a conflict against France.**

731. France gathered its own allies. **Its main ally was the declining Russian Empire.**

732. **France and Russia signed an agreement in 1891 and had an alliance three years later.** The French lent the Russians a lot of funds to rebuild and modernize their infrastructure and military.

733. **Germany increased its military and economy to the point that it seriously challenged Great Britain,** which had emerged as the de facto hegemon of 19th-century Europe.

734. **Great Britain had the strongest navy, an extensive system of colonies, a powerful military, and a large economy.** It also enjoyed an isolated policy, so it was not as affected by the politics of continental Europe.

735. **With Germany's rise to prominence, British foreign policy changed,** with the nation signing agreements with France and Russia.

736. **Britain, Russia, and France formed the Triple Entente to balance against the Triple Alliance.**

737. **The Berlin Conference (1884–1885) saw all of the major powers of Europe come to the negotiating table to discuss the future of Europe** and the rest of the world.

738. **It kicked off the Scramble for Africa, a race to claim lands and colonize Africa,** which was still largely unexplored by Europeans at that time.

739. **The Berlin Conference did not involve drawing arbitrary borders on a map of Africa. Instead,** it formalized existing colonial claims and sought to establish guidelines for future territorial acquisitions.

740. **At the start of the Scramble for Africa, only 10 percent of African land had been claimed by Europeans.** By 1900, that figure had risen to 90 percent.

741. **Many African tribes were forced out or enslaved during this period,** leading to significant loss of life on both sides due to wars fought over territories.

742. **European colonists brought their own culture, language, religion, laws, and education system** into the regions they occupied, replacing the traditional ways of doing things.

743. **France was very active during this period. It acquired more land than any other European nation in West Africa.**

744. **Great Britain was the dominant power in southern Africa. It acquired colonies in Nigeria, Sudan, Uganda, and Kenya.**

745. **Portugal established its colony in Angola, and Italy took control of Libya.**

746. **Germany was late to enter the Scramble for Africa, but it acquired Togoland** (now part of Ghana), Cameroon, and German East Africa (Rwanda and Burundi).

747. **The European empires justified their ruthless conquest and colonization of the African continent** with the belief they were brining enlightenment and progress to the uncivilized parts of the world.

748. **Millions of Africans suffered under brutal colonial rule.** Many were forced to move from their homes, and they experienced terrible living conditions.

749. **The Scramble for Africa led to economic suffering,** as Britain and other countries took resources from colonies with no intention of providing fair trading opportunities.

750. **This period saw the rise of nationalistic feelings among people all over the continent who wanted freedom from colonial rule.** Several independence movements took place after WWI.

751. **Many African countries still suffer from economic inequality and political unrest.** Many political scholars believe this is because of the Scramble for Africa.

752. **The Scramble for Africa shaped much of the current international law governing relations between different states** regarding issues like land rights and resource extraction.

753. **The Scramble for Africa stimulated rivalries between European superpowers,** especially between Germany, France, and Britain.

754. **The British-German rivalry would lead to a naval arms race,** with the newly created German navy challenging the supremacy of **the British Royal Navy** by 1914.

755. **Austria-Hungary slowly absorbed the Balkan nation-states,** which would try to gain their independence from the crumbling Ottoman Empire.

The Balkan Wars
(1912–1913)

The Balkan Wars were a pivotal period in the history of southeastern Europe. Let's unpack twenty facts about how these conflicts began and their impact on World War I.

756. **The Balkan Wars were two conflicts fought between 1912 and 1913.** They resulted in the emergence of new Balkan states and the weakening of the Ottoman Empire.

757. **The First Balkan War occurred from October 1912 to May 1913 and involved the Balkan League** (Serbia, Montenegro, Greece, and Bulgaria) **against the Ottoman Empire.**

758. **The main objective of the Balkan League was to expel the Ottoman Empire from the Balkans** and to gain territory in the region where these nationalities had lived for centuries under Ottoman suzerainty.

759. **The Balkan League quickly achieved significant victories against the Ottoman Empire,** capturing territories in present-day Albania, Macedonia, and Thrace.

760. **The Battle of Kumanovo in October 1912 resulted in a decisive victory for the Balkan League against the Ottomans in Macedonia.**

761. **The Siege of Adrianople (Edirne) in November 1912 was a significant military operation by Bulgarian and Serbian forces,** resulting in the capture of the city from the Ottomans.

762. **The Treaty of London was signed on May 30th, 1913,** ending the First Balkan War and recognizing significant territorial gains for the Balkan League states at the expense of **the Ottoman Empire.**

763. **It was brokered by the great powers of Europe to prevent further escalation of the conflict** and maintain stability in the region.

764. **The First Balkan War also resulted in the creation of an independent Albania.**

765. **The Second Balkan War** occurred from June to August 1913 and **involved Bulgaria against its former allies, Serbia, Greece, and Romania.**

766. **The main cause of the Second Balkan War was Bulgaria's dissatisfaction with the territorial gains it achieved in the Treaty of London.** The Bulgarians had hoped to achieve more from the first conflict.

767. **Bulgaria initiated hostilities against its former allies by attacking Serbian and Greek positions in Macedonia** in June 1913.

768. However, **the Serbian army, with support from Greece and Romania, launched a successful counteroffensive against Bulgaria,** pushing Bulgarian forces back.

769. **The Battle of Kresna Gorge in July 1913 was a significant engagement where Serbian and Greek forces defeated Bulgarian forces** attempting to advance into Greek territory.

770. **Bulgaria was forced to surrender, signing the Treaty of Bucharest on August 10th,** 1913, ending the Second Balkan War. Bulgaria suffered territorial losses.

771. **The territorial adjustments made in the Treaty of Bucharest included Serbia gaining territory in much of Macedonia,** Greece gaining southern Macedonia, and Romania gaining southern Dobruja.

772. **The Balkan Wars were very important in the context of 20th-century Europe. The conflicts significantly weakened the Ottoman Empire's presence in the Balkans,** paving the way for its eventual collapse during World War I.

773. **The Balkan Wars contributed to the growth of nationalist sentiments among various ethnic groups in the region,** leading to further conflicts and tensions in the following decades.

774. **The Balkan Wars resulted in significant population movements,** including the displacement of Muslim populations from territories captured by **the Balkan League states.**

775. **These conflicts are often seen as a prelude to World War I,** as they highlighted the complex web of alliances and rivalries in Europe.

World War I
(1914–1918)

This chapter will explore the events and facts surrounding World War I. We'll look at thirty interesting facts about how it started, the major participants, and major battles. **Discover how WWI changed history forever!**

776. The war began on July 28th, 1914, when **Austria declared war against Serbia in response to the assassination of Archduke Franz Ferdinand.**

777. **Archduke Franz Ferdinand and his wife were assassinated during their visit to the Bosnian city of Sarajevo by Serbian nationalist Gavrilo Princip.**

778. **Serbs, Bosnians, Croats, and other Balkan peoples who had been under the conservative rulership of the Austro-Hungarian Empire were discontent with Habsburg rule.** They wanted independence, and some went to extremes to achieve their goals.

779. **The assassination of Archduke Franz Ferdinand was followed by a series of diplomatic maneuvers by European nations.** This period was known as **the July Crisis,** during which time European countries mobilized their forces and prepared for war.

780. **Russia came in to defend Serbia, causing Austria to declare war on Russia,** which dragged in France, Germany, and Great Britain.

781. **World War I would be the largest war fought by any state at that point in history.**
782. **The total number of casualties was around forty million.** There were around twenty million deaths and twenty-one million wounded. This number includes both civilians and military personnel.

783. **The Ottoman Empire joined the war in 1915 on the side of the Central Powers** (Germany and Austria-Hungary). **The Ottomans** wanted to save their declining empire and take control of territories in the Balkans and the Caucasus.

784. **Italy and the United States sided with the Entente.** Bulgaria joined the war on the side of the Central Powers.

785. **World War I would be so destructive because of the implementation of new tactics and military technologies,** like tanks, airplanes, and machine guns.

786. **World War I became infamous for trench warfare.** Soldiers would dig trench systems on the battlefield, leading to well-fortified defensive positions that would be extremely costly for the other side to attack.

787. **Poison gas was used for the first time in WWI.** By the end of the conflict, more than 125,000 tons of poisonous gases had been released into trenches.

788. **On the Western Front, where Germany fought the British and French,** the largest battles took place at the Somme and Verdun, resulting in more than 1.5 million casualties.

789. **The Battle of Verdun lasted for three hundred days! It was known as the bloodiest battle in WWI,** as there were more than 300,000 French and German losses.

790. **After initial German advances in 1914 and 1915, the French and the British contained the German invasion,** leading to a stalemate that would be broken in 1917 with the arrival of American soldiers.

791. **On December 25th, 1914, British and German soldiers declared a temporary ceasefire.** They exchanged gifts with each other and played a game of football. This day is known as the Christmas Truce.

792. **On the Eastern Front, the German and Austrian forces pushed back the Russian soldiers,** leading to and chaos in Russia.

793. **The Russian Revolution in 1917 saw Russia exit the war.** The revolutionaries also overthrew the Russian Empire.

794. **In 1915, the Allies launched a naval invasion of the Ottoman Empire.** They landed on the Gallipoli Peninsula, hoping to take Constantinople.

795. **The Gallipoli Campaign would last for ten months and result in about 500,000 casualties by mid-1916.** The Allies were unable to break through the Ottoman defenses.

796. **After Italy's entry into the war, the Italians tried to break through into Austria but were met with fierce resistance from Austro-German** forces in modern-day Slovenia on the Isonzo River.

797. **There would be twelve battles along the Isonzo River.** The Italians were pushed from the river in October 1917.

798. **The United States joined WWI in 1917 after German U-boats sunk several American merchant ships** carrying supplies for Allied forces without any warning or prior notice.

799. **Germany was the only Central Power that had an abundance of resources and a competent military throughout most of the war.** The Austrian, Ottoman, and Bulgarian troops lacked discipline and equipment.

800. **As the war dragged on, public sentiment in Berlin and other major German cities** made it impossible to continue the war effort.

801. **The war officially ended with the signing of the Treaty of Versailles on June 28th, 1919.** The treaty placed severe restrictions on Germany for starting the war, including heavy reparations.

802. **Other separate treaties would be signed by the defeated powers in addition to the Treaty of Versailles.**

803. **World War I marked the end of old-fashioned empires in Europe, as Germany, Austria-Hungary, and the Ottoman Empire were reorganized into new states.** The Russian Revolution put an end to the Russian Empire.

804. **The war led to the formation of multiple new nation-states around Europe, such as Czechoslovakia, Hungary, Poland, Ukraine, Georgia, Yugoslavia, and Romania,** where mostly liberal democratic regimes were established.

805. **American President Woodrow Wilson wanted to avoid the breakout of another massive war.** He helped create an international organization called the League of Nations, which many European nations joined.

The Russian Revolution and the Formation of the USSR (1917)

The Russian Revolution was a major event that greatly impacted Europe. These twenty-five fascinating facts will give you a glimpse into what led to the revolution in the first place and the figures who were involved in overthrowing the Russian Empire.

806. **The Russian Revolution began in 1917 amidst World War I** after a series of protests and worker strikes in St. Petersburg and Moscow.

807. **The lower classes dealt with poor living conditions and did not have fundamental rights or economic prosperity.** The protests also began because the Russian forces suffered several defeats in World War I.

808. **As a result of the revolution, the Russian monarch, Tsar Nicholas II,** was forced to abdicate, ending a long line of monarchic succession.

809. **Russia was reorganized into the first communist state in world history.**

810. **The first protests began in March and led to the creation of a provisional government led by the Russian Duma** (the parliamentary body).

811. Local soviets, **socialist workers' councils that governed the affairs of small districts, were also created.**

812. **A group of far-left revolutionaries known as the Bolsheviks grew increasingly influential.** They were led by Vladimir Lenin, an advocate of Marxist principles who believed that communism should be established in Russia.

813. **The Bolsheviks united the local soviets into voluntary armed militias and took control from the provisional government in October.** They established their own government: the Russian Soviet Federative Socialist Republic.

814. **Lenin was supported by Leon Trotsky, who was considered the second in command during the Russian Revolution.** He would be assassinated in 1940 while in exile in Mexico.

815. **A popular Bolshevik slogan during the revolution was "Peace, land, and bread."**

816. **The Bolsheviks signed a peace agreement with the Germans** in March 1918, exiting WWI.

817. **They implemented a range of policies that were aimed at redistributing land and resources from the wealthy to the poor.**

818. **The Bolsheviks were not unopposed.** Anti-socialist and conservative Russians united against the Bolsheviks, forming **the White Army and beginning the Russian Civil War.**

819. **The Russian Civil War ended in 1923 with the defeat of the Whites and the establishment of a socialist regime in Russia.**

820. After the victory, **the Bolsheviks reorganized themselves into the Communist Party** and continued pushing the communist agenda.

821. **The Communists started to believe they had to spread communism to the rest of the world.** They began to invade many neighboring states, including Ukraine, Moldova, and Georgia, all of which were occupied by the Red Army by 1921.

822. **Russia established the Union of Soviet Socialist Republics** (USSR) in December 1922.

823. **Communist regimes were established in newly occupied states,** and the USSR eventually grew to include fifteen members.

824. **The Communist Party took control of all aspects of society after Lenin's death in 1924,** including factories, farms, and schools. It created a one-party state where it held absolute power over the citizens.

825. **After Lenin's death, a young Communist by the name of Joseph Stalin came to power as the head of the Communist Party and the USSR.** He enforced several radical policies like the collectivization of agriculture, which resulted in millions of deaths due to starvation.

826. **Stalin pushed the one-party rule to a new level.** He began a reign of terror and imprisoned and executed hundreds of thousands who were suspected of being the state's enemies.

827. **Prisoners were forced to work in extreme conditions in hundreds of secret labor camps that were scattered around the USSR.** These prisons were known as gulags.

828. **The Soviet Union's new factories greatly increased domestic production,** though it was mostly weapons.

829. **Strict censorship of all aspects of life was implemented. Newspapers, music, theater, and art** had to go through state channels before being disseminated to the public.

830. **The USSR would push for the spread of communism around the world for decades,** financing many far-left movements in Europe and Asia.

The Interwar Period
(1918–1939)

The interwar period was a transformative time in history when the United States rose as the greatest power in the world. Technology advanced dramatically, and popular culture flourished. Let's examine these changes with thirty interesting facts.

831. **The interwar period refers to the time between World War I and World War II.**

832. **Although this period only lasted for about two decades,** the world underwent dramatic technological, socioeconomic, and political changes.

833. **After the end of WWI, democratic regimes were established throughout Europe,** with the war's victors hoping that conservative monarchies would never return to the continent.

834. **The 1920s were a time of recovery for Europe and the rest of the world.** New European nation-states were still getting their acts together and trying to find their place in the new political world order.

835. **For the most part, this decade was peaceful, with the exception of Soviet expansion** into the Caucasus and the establishment of Soviet republics in Georgia, Armenia, and Azerbaijan.

836. **Technology improved dramatically during this time.** Airplanes became much more powerful and were used more by governments around the world for military purposes or transportation reasons.

837. **Popular culture flourished during this time. Jazz music spread across Europe, and Hollywood films were seen around the globe.**

838. **Artistic movements like Surrealism, Dadaism, and Bauhaus emerged, challenging traditional notions of art and culture** and pushing boundaries in painting, sculpture, literature, and design.

839. **Radio broadcasts allowed people to listen to the news as it happened anywhere in the world!**

840. **Women gained more rights during the interwar period;** some countries even gave women the right to vote for the first time in history.

841. **The League of Nations was founded at this time.** Its purpose was to promote international peace and cooperation among nations.

842. **Despite its noble goals, the League of Nations would fail to become a strong,** respected international organization due to the emergence of new regimes that defied its laws.

843. **By the end of the 1920s, Europe and the rest of the world entered a period of great economic decline called the Great Depression.** It began in 1929 and lasted until the late 1930s. It was one of the worst economic downturns ever recorded and caused major social upheaval all over the world.

844. **Every European nation experienced effects from the Great Depression,** such as severe hyperinflation and high unemployment rates, which led to political instability.

845. **Partially as a response to the economic crisis caused by the Great Depression,** far-right nationalist leaders started to gain traction in Europe.

846. **The first prominent far-right movement was Italian fascism.** This movement was led by a former journalist turned radical politician named Benito Mussolini, who became the prime minister in 1922.

847. **Mussolini and his followers advocated for a strong Italy,** and they were ready to use violence against groups they opposed, like liberals or socialists.

848. **Similar developments took place in Germany,** which was renamed the Weimar Republic.

849. **Germany was hit the hardest by the Great Depression,** so public sentiment for revanchism (revenge) was very strong.

850. **Adolf Hitler, inspired by Mussolini's success in Italy,** came to power in 1933 and soon emerged as the dictator of Germany.

851. **His National Socialist German Workers' Party** (the Nazi Party) celebrated the superiority of the German race and stressed the importance of German rearmament and the glory of the German nation.

852. During the 1930s, **Hitler was successful in annexing Austrian and Czechoslovakian territories.** The leaders of democratic regimes in France and Great Britain reluctantly allowed aggressive German expansion.

853. **Italy and Germany formed the Axis, spreading far-right propaganda, usurping all power in the countries,** overpowering the rule of law, and investing heavily in remilitarization.

854. **Fascism became a powerful ideology,** with its proponents pushing for totalitarian control over all aspects of the state and inspiring similar movements all throughout the world.

855. **Fascism would lead to the breakout of the Spanish Civil War** (1936–1939) between those favoring a republic and those wanting a dictatorship.

856. **The Spanish Civil War ended in a victory for the Spanish fascists, who received a lot of help from Italians and Germans.** Francisco Franco would emerge as the dictator of Spain.

857. **The Soviet Union underwent radical changes under the leadership of Joseph Stalin,** who pushed for economic and social reforms.

858. **Stalin's policies were much like those of his totalitarian colleagues in Italy and Germany.** The majority of the Soviet Union's population struggled to overcome poverty and obtain basic living conditions.

859. **Several major international conferences took place during this period, including the Washington Naval Conference** (1921–1922), which sought to limit global armament levels. The Geneva Disarmament Conference (1932–1934) was aimed at reducing military spending by countries.

860. **Although the Soviets and Nazis claimed to be each other's enemies,** the two would agree to a secret plan to invade Poland together in August 1939.

World War II
(1939-1945)

From the Battle of Britain to the bombing of Hiroshima and Nagasaki, World War II was one of the most devastating conflicts in human history. In this chapter, we will explore thirty interesting facts about this influential war.

861. **World War II was the deadliest conflict in human history to date,** with around seventy-five million people killed worldwide.

862. **It started on September 1st, 1939, when Nazi Germany invaded Poland. France and the United Kingdom declared war on Germany in response.**

863. The two main factions in the war would be **the Axis (Germany, Italy and Japan)** and **the Allies (Britain, France, China, the USSR, and the US).**

864. **Germany invaded and defeated Norway and Denmark in 1940.** The Germans also launched an invasion of France through Belgium, the Netherlands, and Luxembourg.

865. **The Nazis occupied Paris on June 14th, 1940, not one year after the beginning of the war.** France signed an armistice with Germany, and the country was organized into occupation zones controlled by the Germans and the Italians.

866. **Great Britain, led by Prime Minister Winston Churchill, organized an amazing defense of the English Channel to stop the Germans from crossing and invading Britain.**

867. **The Battle of Britain was a significant air battle between the German Luftwaffe and the British Royal Air Force in 1940 over control of UK airspace.** Most major British cities, including London, were ruthlessly bombed.

868. **Hitler prepared and launched Operation Barbarossa,** which was intended to be a quick offensive against the Soviet Union in June 1941.

869. **The Soviet military was unable to respond effectively in time.** The Germans made great headway into the Soviet territories and took control of Ukraine, Belarus, and western Russia very quickly.

870. **The Soviets were able to mobilize in time to defend Moscow and Leningrad.** The Germans had to halt their invasion after exhausting their resources.

871. **Japan attacked Pearl Harbor on December 7th, 1941,** bringing **the United States officially into World War II on the side of the Allies.**

872. **The Battle of Stalingrad** (1942–1943) **saw some of the most brutal fighting during WWII.** It was a major turning point, as Nazis started to be pushed back from the Eastern Front.

873. **By the end of 1943, the German offensive into the Soviet Union had been completely halted.** The Germans organized a tactical retreat the following year after a renewed Soviet offensive.

874. **D-Day** (June 6th, 1944) **marked the beginning of the Allied victory in Europe,** with around 160,000 troops landing on five beaches in Normandy, France, to fight the Nazis.

875. **The Allies were not only successful in Normandy but also managed to launch an invasion of Italy from the Mediterranean** in 1943, taking most of southern Italy.

876. **The Allies and the Soviets closed in from the West and the East,** taking Berlin in the spring of 1945.

877. On April 30th, 1945, **Hitler committed suicide in his bunker before Allied troops could find him.**

878. **The Japanese would surrender in the autumn of 1945 after the US dropped two atomic bombs on Hiroshima and Nagasaki,** killing hundreds of thousands at once.

879. **Scientists from Europe, primarily from the United Kingdom, were involved in the Manhattan Project,** which developed the atomic bomb.

880. **When the Allies advanced into German territories, they unraveled the terrible truth the Nazis** had been hiding from the outside world: the mass murder, deportation, and imprisonment of Jews and other minorities.

881. **The Nazis organized forced labor camps in which millions of innocents perished in one of the most tragic events in history.** This event is known as the Holocaust.

882. **The genocide was justified as being part of the "Final Solution,"** which sought to establish the cultural and social dominance of the Aryan race at the expense of inferior races.

883. **The tragedy of the Holocaust is remembered thanks to the accounts of those who lived during it, like Anne Frank, who wrote her diary while hiding from Nazis during WWII.** Her diary became an iconic nonfiction book that teaches us about the horrors inflicted upon innocent people due to war and prejudice.

884. **Women worldwide took on roles as nurses, pilots,** or factory workers for their respective countries since many men were away fighting.

885. **WWII saw some major advances in technology,** including jet aircraft, radar, computers, and atomic weapons, which changed warfare forever.

886. **Bletchley Park, a country estate in England, was the site of a top-secret codebreaking operation during World War II.** The team of **codebreakers**, which included **Alan Turing**, played a crucial role in deciphering **German Enigma machine codes**.

887. **Poland's capital, Warsaw, was completely destroyed during the war.**

888. **Winston Churchill was the prime minister of the United Kingdom during WWII.** He is remembered as one of the greatest leaders in history. He helped lead his country to victory against Nazi Germany through his inspirational speeches and strategy-planning skills.

889. **The United Nations (UN) replaced the League of Nations as a global peacekeeping organization after WWII ended.** Its goal was the prevention of another large-scale war and the establishment of a new world order.

890. **Stalin occupied most of Eastern Europe and established communist regimes in countries like Poland, Romania, Czechoslovakia, and East Germany.**

The Cold War
(1945–1991)

From 1945 to 1991, the world witnessed an intense rivalry between two superpowers: the United States and the Soviet Union. Known as the **"Cold War,"** this period was characterized by a race for political influence in Europe, Asia, and Africa. In this chapter, we will explore twenty interesting facts about **the Cold War.**

891. **The Cold War was a time of tension between the United States and the Soviet Union** that lasted from 1945 to 1991.

892. **Both countries wanted to be the most powerful and spread their ideologies around the world,** which led to competition for political influence in places like Europe, Asia, and Africa.

893. **The Cold War led to a huge arms race where both powers built up their military arsenals** in an attempt to gain superiority over each other.

894. **Each side developed nuclear weapons during this period** as a deterrent against attack by the other side, but these were never used in combat.

895. **Instead of fighting directly with each other, they fought proxy wars, like in Vietnam or Korea,** where both sides supported different sides in a conflict without actually entering into direct battle themselves.

896. **Throughout the Cold War, Eastern European states were under heavy Soviet influence.** Puppet communist regimes spread anti-Western propaganda and limited the freedoms of their citizens.

897. In March 1946, **Winston Churchill said in a speech that an Iron Curtain had descended upon Europe,** symbolizing the split between democratic and communist European states.

898. **This rivalry led to space exploration. Each country competed for superiority in technology and science.** Russia launched **Sputnik 1,** the first artificial satellite ever sent into orbit.

899. From 1948 to 1949, **the Soviet Union blockaded West Berlin, cutting off all land and water routes to the city.** In response, the West organized the Berlin Airlift, a massive airlift operation to supply West Berlin with food, fuel, and other essentials. The airlift lasted for eleven months.

900. **The Cold War saw huge growth in international organizations like NATO and the United Nations,** which were formed to prevent future wars.

901. **Important documents, such as the Helsinki Accords, were signed during this time,** outlining agreements on how different countries would treat each other politically and economically while respecting human rights.

902. **European democracies began their process of economic and political integration in the 1950s during the Cold War** in an effort to prevent another conflict from breaking out in Europe.

903. **Many people escaped communist rule through defections or emigration,** seeking refuge in countries like the United States and Canada.

904. **The Cold War deescalated in 1989 when the Berlin Wall** (a physical divide between East and West Germany) **was torn down.**

905. **Ultimately, the Cold War ended with a victory for democracy and free markets,** as communist regimes eventually collapsed in Europe by the 1990s.

Decolonization
(1945–the 1960s)

This chapter will explore the significant period of decolonization that occurred between 1945 and the 1960s. These fifteen facts will cover some of the countries that achieved independence and what changes were made.

906. **Decolonization is the process of countries gaining independence from being colonies of other,** usually larger and more powerful nations.

907. **The start of decolonization began in 1945 at the end of World War II** when many European nations gave up their colonies as a result of losing power and money during the war.

908. **In 1947, India became an independent nation after centuries under British rule.**

909. **Many African nations gained independence between the mid-1950s and 1975,** with Ghana becoming the first sub-Saharan country to do so in 1957.

910. **Decolonization happened in Oceania, with Papua New Guinea achieving independence from Australia in 1975** and **Samoa** gaining independence from **New Zealand** just one year later.

911. **During decolonization, many countries had to fight for their freedom,** while others obtained it through peaceful negotiations and agreements with former colonial powers.

912. **A particularly violent example of decolonization in Africa is Algeria,** which fought a brutal war against the **French** from 1954 to 1962, leading to the death and displacement of millions of people.

913. **The process of decolonization was often accompanied by civil wars,** as groups within a newly independent nation fought over power or ideologies.

914. **The United Nations played an important role in helping facilitate these new nations'** diplomatic recognition, economic aid, and peacekeeping operations.

915. **In some instances, former colonies were so financially unstable that they had to rely on foreign powers for support,** leading to what is known as "neocolonialism," which is when a country appears independent but still has strong economic ties with its colonizer.

916. **Decolonization led to population displacement** as many people left newly formed nations due to political instability or a lack of resources or employment opportunities.

917. **Decolonization encouraged the idea that all people should be treated equally** regardless of their race or religion, paving the way for **civil rights movements.**

918. **The decolonization of nations led to an increase in international commerce,** as the newly independent states started to establish links with foreign nations that had previously been under colonial rule.

919. **Education initiatives were developed as part of this process, allowing citizens from former colonies to gain access to higher education for the first time.**

920. **During this period, there were significant changes in culture.** For instance, newly formed countries declared other languages as the official language than the one used by their   colonizers.

The Prague Spring
(1968)

The Prague Spring of 1968 was a period of mass protest in Czechoslovakia. In this chapter, we will explore fifteen facts about this pivotal event in history.

921. **The Prague Spring was a period of political liberalization and reform in Czechoslovakia** (now the Czech Republic and Slovakia) that lasted from January to August 1968.

922. **It started with reforms led by Alexander Dubcek,** the leader of the Communist Party.

923. **These reforms included more freedom for citizens,** such as relaxed censorship laws, fewer restrictions on travel abroad, and greater economic freedoms.

924. **Thousands of people gathered in Wenceslas Square in Prague** (the capital city) to show their support for Dubcek's efforts and demand greater reforms to be taken by the government.

925. **This was seen as a threat by the USSR. Moscow** saw the Czechoslovakian government as its puppet and did not want liberal reforms.

926. In April 1968, **five communist states—Bulgaria, Hungary, Poland, East Germany, and the Soviet Union—sent troops into Czechoslovakia** to end what they saw as dangerous developments toward democracy.

927. **According to some reports, about 650,000 troops entered Czechoslovakia** in response to the gathered public in April 1968.

928. On August 21st, 1968, **Dubcek announced an agreement that allowed some limited f reform but prohibited the regime's further liberalization.**

929. **This agreement was known as the Prague Spring** because it ended the period of reform and brought back tight communist control.

930. In 1969, **Dubcek was removed from office and replaced by a hardline communist leader who restricted some of his reforms, ending the Prague Spring.**

931. **After the invasion, Czechoslovakian officials pushed for a policy of normalization,** which meant a return to the status quo before the protests.

932. **The Prague Spring was seen as an inspiration to other countries in the Eastern Bloc,** with some of its reforms being adopted by Hungary and Poland.

933. **In 1989, the Velvet Revolution peacefully overthrew the government that had been in power since 1948,** restoring democracy to Czechoslovakia for good this time.

934. To this day, **the Prague Spring remains an important moment of freedom and hope** for those struggling against oppressive regimes.

935. **It became a source of inspiration for many prominent Czech authors, such as Milan Kundera and Vaclav Havel,** who emerged as influential voices against Communist oppression.

The Fall of the Berlin Wall
(1989)

This chapter will explore the remarkable story of the fall of the Berlin Wall in 1989. We'll discover twenty incredible facts about the history of the Berlin Wall and why it was finally removed.

936. **The Berlin Wall was a physical barrier between East and West Germany. It was built in 1961 to separate the two during the Cold War.**

937. After the end of WWII, **Berlin had been divided by the Allies and the Soviet Union** into democratic West Berlin and communist East Berlin.

938. **East Berliners would regularly cross to West Berlin,** where life was much more prosperous and freer compared to the East.

939. **East Germany spread the idea that a democratic capitalist regime was an inferior way to live compared to communism.**

940. After 1961, **crossing to West Berlin without an official permit was not allowed.** East German guards were instructed to shoot anyone who tried to move to the other side.

941. **Many people still tried to cross to the West,** partly to escape the communist rule and partly to smuggle goods to the East.

942. **Around 140 people died trying to cross the Berlin Wall between 1961 and 1989.** It is possible the number was much higher.

943. **East Germans dug tunnels under the wall, hid in vehicles, or disguised themselves as border guards to get past the wall.** Some even used hot air balloons or ziplines to cross the border.

944. **The Berlin Wall stood for twenty-eight years.**

945. On November 9th, 1989, **the East German government unexpectedly announced that citizens could freely travel to the West.** Crowds of East Berliners gathered at the Berlin Wall, and border guards eventually opened the checkpoints.

946. **As news spread of the opening of the Berlin Wall, crowds began to gather on both sides,** armed with hammers, chisels, and other tools to chip away at the concrete barrier. People climbed onto the wall, singing, dancing, and celebrating the end of division and the reunification of Germany.

947. On December 22nd, 1989, **West German Chancellor Helmut Kohl and East German Prime Minister Hans Modrow signed an agreement** to begin dismantling the wall.

948. **The Brandenburg Gate became renowned as a representation of liberation once Germany was reunited;** this historic landmark had been restricted from public access by East German troops since 1961.

949. **In June 1990, after months of negotiations between East and West Germany,** Germany officially reunited into a single nation.

950. **The reunification is now commemorated on October 3rd each year,** with celebrations across Germany, including fireworks displays over the former Berlin Wall site at Potsdamer Platz.

951. **Parts of the Berlin Wall still stand to this day,** serving as a memorial and as a popular tourist destination.

952. **The graffiti painted on either side by protesters has become part of the open-air museum experience.**

953. **In 1963, American President John F. Kennedy visited West Berlin and gave his famous "Ich bin ein Berliner" speech,** in which he addressed the injustice experienced by the inhabitants of Berlin and criticized the USSR and its communist satellites for erecting a physical barrier in the city.

954. **On the thirtieth anniversary of the fall, a light installation was erected on the former Berlin Wall site to commemorate its history.**

955. **Although the reunification of Germany was largely peaceful,** it did take a long time for both sides to adjust economically and politically.

The Yugoslav Wars
(1991–2001)

Explore the devastating conflicts of the Yugoslav Wars. In this chapter, we'll explore fifteen interesting facts about this tumultuous period in history, including how many people lost their lives and how many were forced to flee.

956. **The Yugoslav Wars were a series of wars that happened between 1991 and 2001 in the area known as Yugoslavia,** which is now made up of several countries, including Croatia, Serbia, and Bosnia and Herzegovina, among others.

957. **The ethnic groups that made up the state of Yugoslavia declared their independence in 1991,** and their revolutionary movements eventually turned into full-on conflicts.

958. **The wars were caused mostly due to political reasons stimulated by historic ethnic conflicts over territory** among different peoples living in the region who had their own languages and religions.

959. **Between 140,000 and 250,000 people died from fighting** or related causes like starvation or disease during the war.

960. **Millions of people were forced to leave their homes** because of violence or fear for their safety.

961. **The war between Serbia and Croatia, which lasted from 1991 to 1995,** was especially deadly, resulting in up to thirty thousand casualties.

962. **Bosnia and Herzegovina had a terrible civil war** that took place from 1992 to 1995.

963. **NATO** (the North Atlantic Treaty Organization) **got involved by providing air strikes against Serbian forces** and ground troops for peacekeeping missions during the wars.

964. **The International Criminal Tribunal for the Former Yugoslavia (ICTY) was established in 1993** to bring justice to those who committed serious violations of international humanitarian law during these wars.

965. **To help people affected by the conflict, various UN agencies and NGOs** (non-governmental organizations) **provided medical care, food aid, and other forms of assistance.**

966. **The wars had a huge impact on Yugoslavia's economy;** it lost over $100 billion during this period.

967. **Many cultural monuments were destroyed or damaged during the Yugoslav Wars. Among them was the city of Dubrovnik,** which was heavily damaged during a siege by the Yugoslav People's Army from October 1991 to May 1992.

968. The use of propaganda was common. **Newspapers were used to spread false information about opposing groups,** and leaders tried to influence public opinion through speeches or interviews given to media outlets.

969. **Some countries around Europe closed their borders while others,** like Sweden, offered asylum for those fleeing the war zones.

970. **The Yugoslav Wars are described as the bloodiest conflict in Europe since the end of World War II in 1945,** marked by many war crimes and crimes against humanity, which earned it its infamous reputation.

The European Union
(1951—Present)

For centuries, the European Union has been a driving force for peace and progress in Europe. Since its founding, it has grown to become one of today's largest economies. This chapter will explore thirty-five fascinating facts about the EU.

971. **The European Union is a multinational political and economic union of European states,** which emerged throughout the second half of the 20th century.

972. **Belgium, France, Italy, Luxembourg, the Netherlands, and West Germany were the original six countries that began the process of European integration** with the creation of the European Coal and Steel Community in 1951.

973. **Over the next decades, these countries decided to expand their economic and political ties,** creating more shared institutions that benefitted the practice of the rule of law and the development of democratic regimes.

974. **The European countries then decided to unite together into a large supranational political entity to pursue the same goals.** They adopted the name "European Union" in the 1990s.

975. **The organization expanded slowly, with the UK, Ireland, and Denmark joining in 1973 to the European Economic Community (EEC)** – the organization that would be transformed into the European Union in the 1990s.

976. **The number of member states rose to fifteen before the end of the 20th century.**

977. Today, **the EU is composed of twenty-seven member states.** It is likely the number of nation-states will increase in the following years.

978. **Each member country has its own government,** but they work together to make decisions that benefit all members of the EU.

979. **English, French, and German are the most commonly used languages in EU meetings,** although other languages are also used depending on which country hosts them.

980. **The headquarters of the EU is in Brussels, Belgium.** This is where most of the main buildings and offices are located, including their parliament building in the European Quarter of Brussels.

981. Since its creation, **the EU has managed to develop a system of free movement of goods, services, labor, and capital.**

982. **Traveling and doing business between the member states of the EU is very easy,** although there are a few restrictions.

983. **The EU has a common market, and many of its countries use the same currency—the euro—** which was introduced in the early 21st century.

984. In 2004, **ten new countries joined the EU: the Czech Republic, Estonia, Hungary, Latvia, Lithuania, Malta, Poland, Cyprus, Slovenia, and Slovakia.**

985. **Bulgaria and Romania joined the EU in 2007.**

986. **In 2009, Croatia became the twenty-eighth country to join the EU,** opening up further opportunities for trade between its neighboring economies.

987. **In 2016, the British public voted to leave the European Union in a referendum.** This decision was dubbed **"Brexit."**

988. **The EU is involved in almost all aspects of life in Europe,** including trade, travel, tourism, the environment, and justice.

989. **It helps protect people's rights, such as the freedom of speech and the right to privacy,** by introducing laws and policies that apply to all member states.

990. **The EU does not interfere in the national decisions its member states make; rather,** it dictates the general direction of domestic and foreign policy and makes it easier for the member states to engage in economic relations.

991. **The European Union provides financial assistance to member states that are struggling with their economies** or need help with development projects like building roads or schools.

992. **This money comes from taxes paid by citizens within each country,** which are then redistributed amongst other members when needed.

993. Each year, **there has been an official "Europe Day" celebrated on May 9th since 1985.** This date was chosen because it marks the anniversary of when Robert Schuman, a French politician, proposed the idea of a united Europe in 1950.

994. **The EU is involved in many foreign affairs and has international relations with other countries around the world like China and the US.** The EU helps to broker peace deals between conflicting states and provides aid where needed.

995. **It also has its own anthem called "Ode to Joy" by Ludwig van Beethoven,** which was adopted by the member states in 1985.

996. **Every five years, there are national elections for members of the European Parliament** (MEPs). The MEPs represent each country within the EU on issues that affect everyone, such as climate change or security policy reform.

997. **The EU is one of the world's largest economies, with a GDP** (gross domestic product) **of more than $20 trillion in 2019.**

998. **It has its own court of justice called the European Court of Justice,** which deals with legal disputes between member states or individuals within Europe.

999. **The Schengen Area is a zone of European countries that have abolished passports and other types of border control at their mutual borders.** The Schengen Agreement, signed in 1985, has been incorporated into EU law.

1000. **The EU has been presented with many domestic and international challenges,** such as **the migrant crisis in the 2010s** when it had to deal with an influx of an exceptionally large number of migrants from **the Middle East.**

Conclusion

In this book, we have explored European history from the Upper Paleolithic period to the present day. It is remarkable to think of the great leaps and bounds that European civilization has seen in the past forty thousand years.

We have looked at the transition from hunter-gatherer societies to early **civilizations in the Mediterranean,** the emergence of empires, and the development of complex political, economic, and social systems. We have examined how **the Industrial Revolution and the two world wars reshaped Europe and how the Cold War divided the continent for decades.** We have also seen how **the European Union** was formed and the impact it has had on **European politics, economics, and culture**. Finally, we have discussed more recent events, such as **the Yugoslav Wars** and the creation of the EU.

This book has provided an overview of many of the most important events and moments in European history and has shown how these moments have shaped the continent as we know it today. It is clear that **European history is a complex, fascinating, and ever-evolving narrative,** and we can only hope that the future of Europe holds many more exciting stories to tell.

Part 2: European History Stories

50 True and Fascinating Tales of Major Events and People from Europe's Past

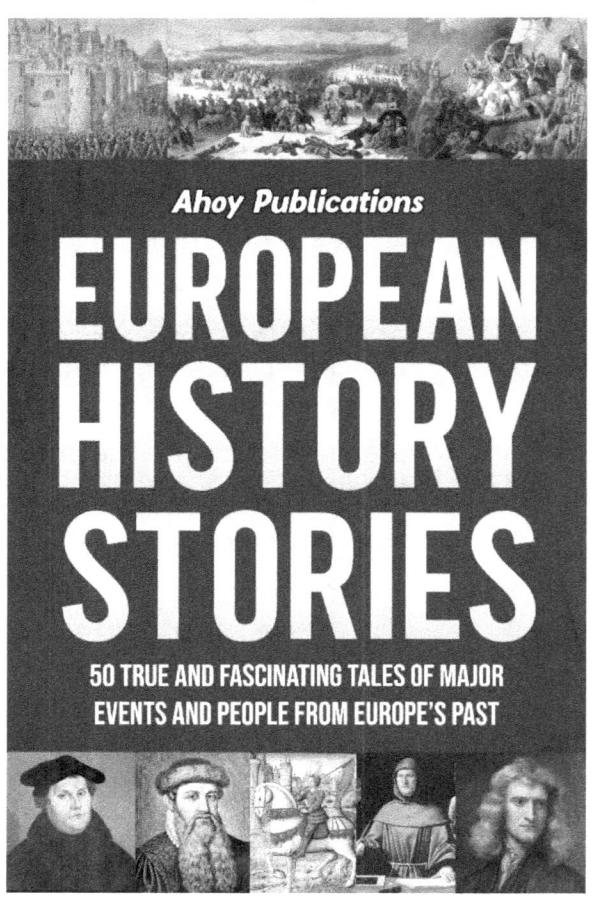

Introduction

You will embark on a journey through the chronicles of history as you read this book. You'll find captivating stories full of triumphs, challenges, and tribulations. This book explores key historical moments that have shaped the modern world using comprehensive, enlightening narratives that bridge the past, present, and future. What sets this book apart is that it offers an extensive view of European history, spanning different periods.

From the birth of democracy in Athen's Agora to the Holocaust, this book delves into transformative, enlightening, inspiring, and devastating historical moments. You will traverse the rise and fall of empires in Europe, the emergence and spread of religions, the outburst of revolutions, and the exploits of rulers and explorers. The stories of prominent individuals and historical events, along with the profound effects and consequences of their doings, will unfold in each chapter.

Your journey will take off in the birthplace of democracy: Ancient Greece. You'll learn about the structure of the nation's city-states and gain insight into the societal reforms that gave rise to democracy. The book illustrates the pros and cons of this political system and explains the roles of the citizenry, along with other political components, in the enduring legacy of Athenian democracy.

The book will then guide you through Julius Caesar's early life, his ascent to power, and notable achievements, leading you all the way to his assassination and enduring influence on the Roman Empire and beyond. You'll then learn how Christianity spread in Europe, trace the early Christian communities, and dive into the world of missionary journeys and the challenges that arose along the way.

You'll dig into the realm of Norsemen and Vikings, their motivations and remarkable journeys, and the far-reaching influence they left in Europe. Your expedition will take a harrowing turn as you learn about the Black Death, its origins, how it spread, and its life-altering consequences.

Fortunately, the book will pick up a more upbeat tone as it steers you toward the Renaissance and the influence of prominent families on the culture, politics, and economics of the time. You'll jump into the Age of Exploration and uncover the narratives of explorers like Columbus, da Gama, and Magellan as they navigated new horizons, leading to the rise of colonial empires.

You'll embrace the Age of Enlightenment and learn about the interesting philosophical ideas of Voltaire, Rousseau, and Kant and their influence on notable revolutions. You'll then discover Napoleon Bonaparte's extraordinary journey from obscurity to absolute power and explore his military successes and the lasting impact his efforts had on Europe. Finally, you'll encounter the distressing legacy of Hitler, reading into his rise and rule and the calamities he inflicted.

Chapter 1: Stories from Ancient Greece

This chapter explores the rich tapestry of ancient Greece's social, political, and philosophical life that led to the birth of democracy. It delves into the structure of the city-state, uncovering its landmarks and unique governance and focusing on Athens as the beacon of early democratic practice. Reading this chapter, you'll understand how democracy emerged and learn about the societal reforms that made it possible.

You'll learn about the benefits and drawbacks of the Athenian democracy and how it affected individuals and society at large. You'll learn about the roles of the citizenry, the Assembly, the Council of Five Hundred, and how their decisions guided Athenian life. Finally, the chapter uncovers how the legacy of Athenian democracy is significant to modern democratic principles.

1. The Structure of the City-State

Ancient Greece comprised numerous city-states, known as polis, which set down the community structure. Each polis had an urban center, protected by walls and surrounded by rural grounds. While all of them were in the same nation, each city-state had its own governing laws. All urban centers were home to government buildings and temples, usually built on a hill known as an acropolis. The Athenian Parthenon, built in honor of Athena, the goddess of wisdom, is an example of an acropolis. The cities were rich in culture and political activities and

Ancient Greece was made up of numerous city-states.[1]

served as the center of commerce and trade, which is why they were home to the majority of the population.

Although there were over 1000 ancient Greek city-states, Athens, Sparta, Thebes, Aegina, Corinth, Syracuse, Eretria, Rhodes, Argos, and Elis were the 10 main ones. Each polis' ruling style, philosophies, and way of life were unique. For instance, while Athenians were known for their love of art and knowledge, Sparta was characterized by its strong military and government. Greece's geography and physical features were likely among the reasons why this community and political structure were developed. The mountains and rocky terrain caused people to form separate and independent communities. The sea was a relatively easier medium of communication than land. Additionally, the aristocrats believed it was easier to spot and eliminate tyrants if they maintained independent city-states rather than a central monarchy.

2. Cleisthenes: The Father of Athenian Democracy

Cleisthenes, the father of Athenian democracy.[2]

The word *democracy* is derived from the term *demokratia*, which refers to a political system influenced by the general public. The first half of the term comes from the word demos, which translates to the people. The other half is derived from kratos, which means power. Cleisthenes developed This political reform system in 507 BC, becoming the world's first-ever democracy.

Demokratia had three components: the ekklesia, the boule, and the dikasteria. The Ekklesia was a sovereign body in the government that wrote laws and foreign policies. They also had the power to practice ostracism, which refers to the act of expelling someone from Athens for a decade. The boule was a council that consisted of representatives from the ten tribes of Athens. The *dikasteria* referred to the courts where citizens took their arguments and presented their cases before jurors. This political invention still shapes the lives of millions of people worldwide millennia later.

One of the greatest achievements that Cleisthenes, the father of democracy, amounted to was that the Athenian aristocrats no longer had autonomous power over political decisions. He also eliminated the distinction between them and the low- and middle-working class who were in the army and navy.

According to Herodotus, Cleisthenes' innovation has made all people equal before the law. In reality, however, this equality didn't apply to the entire ancient Athenian population because only men older than 18 were allowed to participate in democratic procedures. There were around 250,000 citizens in Athena in the 4th century, only 40,000 of whom were men over 18.

3. The Agora: The Heart of Athenian Life and Politics

The Agora lies in the bustling center of ancient Athens. This marketplace captured the essence of ancient Greek life and politics. The Agora, considered the heart of the city-state, was where trade and commerce procedures occurred, and culture and democracy emerged.

The Agora, a busy, open space located at the base of the Acropolis, was the physical hub that gathered the Athenian population. It accommodated a wide range of activities, including many political gatherings, social interactions, and religious rituals. Merchants arrived at the Agora from all over the Mediterranean to trade all kinds of goods, from textiles and pottery to precious metals and spices. This marketplace was crucial to Athens' economic life and was among the most important streams of Greek capital. While most ancient Greek city-states had an Agora, none were as famous or large as the one found in Athens.

The Athenian Agora both directly and indirectly influenced modern-day trade and commerce procedures. Today's online or brick-and-mortar marketplaces still reflect the basic principles of exchange and trade that merchants conducted in the Agora. This ancient marketplace also offers valuable insights and information regarding the development and evolution of early economies, trade practices, and civic life. This might influence how today's economic and political issues are addressed, allowing responsible entities to make informed decisions.

The Agora was not only a marketplace and political hub but also a cultural and intellectual center. There, you can find the Stoa of Attalos, rebuilt in the 20th century. This colonnade used to house numerous schools of philosophy and was where philosophical debates and discussions occurred. The Agora was adorned with sculptures, pottery, and other incredible works of art. Artisans also displayed and traded their masterpieces there. Poets and scholars gathered alongside artists, creating an environment of cultural exchange, beauty, and creativity in the marketplace.

The Agora was also associated with religious life and practices, as it was home to various temples and altars dedicated to numerous deities. The Hephaisteion, a temple that honors the deity Hephaestus, still stands today. Religious rituals, celebrations, sacrifices, and festivals were essential aspects of Athenian traditions and identity – and usually took place in the Agora.

On top of all these functions, the Agora was a place where people could meet and make friends every day. The marketplace offered several food and beverage options, and civilians went there to hang out, engage in discussions, and share news. The Agora is a melting pot, proving that art, social interactions, politics, religion, and commerce can co-exist and thrive together.

4. The Pnyx: Where Democracy Took Center Stage

Jury members often met in the Agora to discuss eminent issues, share their opinions and concerns, and simply bond. This social hub featured a large assembly area, the Pnyx, making the Agora a center of life and politics. Athenian members of the Assembly gathered at the Pnyx to discuss and vote on social and legal issues. The Athenian Agora is particularly historically significant because it was the birthplace of democracy.

The Pros and Cons of Ancient Athenian Democracy
The Pros of the New Political System

• It Increased Political Participation

Ancient Athenian democracy enabled citizens to actively participate in the political process. The portion of citizens who were allowed to partake in these procedures were able to share their opinions, vote and participate in the decision-making process, and propose legislation. Even if the entire population was not involved, the public still felt engaged and had a say in the policies and laws that shaped their lives. This fostered a sense of responsibility and control over their well-being and that of the state.

• It Was More Inclusive

Even if the new democratic system didn't apply to a large portion of the population, Cleisthenes' reforms still encouraged inclusivity because they extended beyond the traditional aristocracy. People who weren't of noble birth could now partake in these decisions, reducing the concentration of power among the nobles. This led to better social cohesion and contributed to the success of the polis.

• It Offered a Degree of Legal Protection

The new democratic system offered legal protection for citizens since it allowed them to seek redress for injustices and disagreements through fair and open trials. Everyone who believed they had been victims of violations was offered a degree of legal resources, enhancing the overall justice system and morale of the society.

The Cons of the New Political System

• It Offered Limited Public Participation

While the political system became more inclusive and encouraged political participation in comparison to earlier exclusively aristocratic systems, it was still very limited. The reforms only included men who fit certain criteria, such as having an Athenian bloodline or serving in the military. Women, slaves, and non-Athenians were excluded from the political system. Even though Cleisthenes' innovation gave more voice to the public, most members of the society couldn't share their opinions or defend and look out for their needs. This may have created further inequalities and marginalized groups within Athenian society.

• It Had the Potential for Demagoguery

Since citizens voted directly on important issues, there was always the possibility of demagogues manipulating public opinion for their own personal gain. They might have also pushed policies that prioritized their personal benefit and weren't in the city-state's long-term interest. The Athenian democracy was direct, making it more vulnerable to demagoguery, which raised concerns regarding the wisdom and stability of this political system.

• It Required a Significant Amount of Time and Resources

Partaking in the democratic political system required significant time and resources. Citizens who wished to vote and participate in the decision-making process had to serve on juries and attend assemblies, putting a strain on their work and family obligations. Those who tried to find a balance between personal and political commitments had limited participation in the democratic process, and those who couldn't dedicate adequate time and resources were excluded.

The Roles of the Citizenry, the Assembly, and the Council of Five Hundred

The citizenry, the Assembly, and the Council of Five Hundred played key roles in the ancient Athenian democratic system. Their contributions to the decision-making process guided all aspects of Athenian life, from daily administration matters to life-changing laws and policies.

The Citizenry

Only males over 18, free, and born to Athenian parents were granted Athenian citizenship after they served in the military for two years. Those who came from other city-states were treated as foreigners, and all women and slaves were excluded from citizenship. Citizens were granted rights and responsibilities in the democratic system and could vote on legislation, participate in the Assembly, and hold public office.

However, to attain and maintain these rights, they were expected to fulfill certain civic duties, such as dedicating the required time and resources to attending the Assembly when needed and serving in the military. The first form of democracy was characterized by its direct nature, where citizens were directly involved in decision-making. They were able to raise important matters and propose, vote, and debate laws and policies that affected the city-state and other members of the society.

5. The Assembly of Athens: The Voice of the People

The Assembly, also known as the Ekklesia, was the main Athenian democratic institution. It served as an open forum where all eligible citizens could meet, discuss, debate, and vote on important matters. However, convicts of self-prostitution, those who owed debt to the treasury, and those who failed to support or beat their family members were denied membership in the Assembly. All decisions made in the Assembly influenced aspects of Athenian life.

The Assembly gathered around 40 times per year at the Pnyx, an open-air auditorium, to address topics that spanned various areas in life, such as foreign policy, laws, financial matters, and the activities of public officials. All citizens could speak and participate in the Assembly, voice their concerns and opinions, and propose legislation, with those over 50 participating first. Major decisions were taken through majority votes, with the votes of all participants being presented and counted.

The Council of Five Hundred

The Council of Five Hundred, or the Boule, was an executive and administrative body that organized and implemented the Assembly's decisions and managed day-to-day affairs. Posting the locations and agendas of upcoming Assembly meetings was among their responsibilities.

The Boule was made up of 500 citizens, which consisted of 50 eligible individuals from the ten territorial units of Athens. Choosing the members was a relatively randomized process to lower the possibility of corruption. Members of this council only served one-year terms and couldn't serve more than twice in their lifetimes. This policy prevented the concentration of power among a few individuals. The Boule had several subcommittees that governed several areas, such as financial affairs, religious matters, and foreign affairs, ensuring the effective administration of the city-state.

How Their Decisions Guided Athenian Life

- Members of the Assembly proposed legislation, passed laws, and addressed policies that influenced daily life in Athens. They made decisions regarding foreign alliances and affairs, social regulations, trade, and taxation. The citizenry's direct involvement shaped the political and social landscapes at the time.

- The Boule ensured that all the decisions made by the Assembly were implemented. Members of this council managed public finances, oversaw the enforcement of laws, and organized military expeditions. They were cornerstones of the effectiveness of this political system.
- The Assembly and the Boule were held accountable to the citizenry. Citizens could practice ostracism or take legal actions against members of the Assembly or the Boule if they had taken unsatisfactory decisions or actions.

The Legacy of Athenian Democracy and Modern Democratic Principles

The Athenian democracy, which shaped the lives of ancient Greek civilians around 2,300 years ago, has served as a significant and everlasting stepping stone of the modern-day political and legal system. The Athenian democratic system has shaped today's democratic principles and practices that are enacted all across the globe. The following are a few ways in which the ancient Athenian democracy is eminent in contemporary democratic political structures:

The Participation and Influence of Citizens

Ancient Athenian democracy was characterized by direct citizen participation in political decision-making, while modern-day systems are more organized and are characterized by the use of representatives. Representatives ensure that citizens actively voice their concerns and participate in democratic processes while lowering the risk of demagoguery and reducing the time and resources that engaging in the political system requires.

While Athenian democracy set criteria for people allowed to participate in the democratic process, the use of representatives nowadays ensures that everyone of legal age can partake in the process. The concept of popular sovereignty, which grants citizens ultimate political authority, also embodies the attributes of Athenian democracy.

Inclusive Political Systems

The shift from allowing only a narrow pool of aristocrats to participate in political decisions to giving power to a larger population segment was huge at the time. This reform laid the foundation for more inclusive political systems that foster civic equality. The fact that many people worldwide can now vote and participate in the legal decision-making process, regardless of their social status or birthplace, is the essence of democracy and was made possible by Cleisthenes' reform. This idea has led to the removal or diminishing of voting barriers, increased civil rights, and the fight against discrimination.

Laws That Reflect the Will of Citizens

Athenian democracy recognized the rule of law, a fundamental principle in democratic legal systems that stresses the importance of accountability, equality, transparency, and the protection of civilian rights. The rule of law holds all individuals accountable and equal before the law and provides fair and just legal processes. This rule also limits the power that the government has, making it crucial for maintaining justice and order and protecting the rights of the people and democratic principles.

Ancient Athenian laws were set forward by the Assembly and applied to all citizens impartially. Contemporary democratic processes continue to reflect the will of citizens and uphold equality and fairness. The ancient Athenian practice of holding government officials accountable through practices like ostracism and other legal actions contributed to the modern-day concept of government accountability and the checks and balances system.

Free Speech and Debate

The Assembly served as a public forum where eligible members could debate their opinions regarding laws and legislation and discuss various matters. Participants freely voted and deliberated on issues of importance. Modern democratic systems also encourage open discourse and free speech. It's believed that the exchange of ideas is vital for social and national welfare.

Grounds for Experimentation

The Athenian democratic model served as grounds for experimenting with democratic governance. Ancient Greek philosophers like Aristotle and Plato also inspired, critiqued, and analyzed Athenian democracy and offered invaluable insights into the strengths and weaknesses of the system. This allowed today's responsible parties to learn from past lessons and experiences and fine-tune them to suit modern life.

Ancient Athenian democracy resulted in lasting influence over global political systems, making them more inclusive and fostering greater political participation and legal protection. The democratic system at the time, however, also had drawbacks that modern entities could learn from. Athenian democracy limited those who could participate in political procedures by setting certain eligibility criteria, demanded significant time and resources, and was susceptible to demagoguery. Ancient Athenian democracy laid the foundation for refined democratic systems that transformed world politics.

Chapter 2: Stories of the Roman Empire

The Roman Empire has commanded the interest and attention of many historians and storytellers for centuries. It is hard to delve into the history of the eternal city without finding yourself caught up in a labyrinth of wonder and awe. Tales of legends, myths, and heroes woven together in the history of the birthplace of the Olympians.

Throughout history, poets, painters, and entertainers have adopted Rome as their muse to express their artistry. It is a fascinating story that never gets old, from its celebrated victories to its tales of woes.

You may ask yourself how this city of hills came to be the world's capital. There is a lot of controversy as to how this city came to life, not to mention the fact that many seem to have a different opinion on when it came to be

Romulus and Remus.[3]

The Foundation of Roma

You may enjoy this tale if you're into mythology and majestic stories! Long ago, around 753 BC, Rome was founded by twin brothers Romulus and Remus.

The brothers were no ordinary humans; they were born of human mothers and fathered by the God of war, Mars. Shortly after their birth, King Amulius ordered their death by being placed in a basket and set free in the Tiber River to die of exposure and starvation.

The God of the River, Tiberinus, calmed the river tide to ensure the children's safety. As fate would have it, their basket would wash up on the river bank, where a female wolf stumbled upon them. The predator, against its own nature, nursed the young cubs until they were found by a shepherd. The shepherd took the children home to his wife, who decided to raise them as their own. Years passed, and the brothers became fit young men helping their adoptive father tend to the sheep. One day, they were confronted by the shepherds of the King, and a fight ensued.

As the stars would have it, they had a hand in defeating and killing the King who had tried to condemn them to death as infants. Time passed, and the twins decided to build a city together at the same spot where their basket had washed up on the Tiber River. Romulus wished to have Rome at the top of the Palatine Hill, while Remus favored the Aventine Hill. After failing to settle the disagreement peacefully, Romulus murdered his brother and fulfilled his wish of laying Rome's foundation on the Palatine Hill, becoming the first Roman King.

Now, if those tales have captured your interest, you should probably brace yourself for the saga of Julius Caesar.

6. From Rubicon to Rome: The Path of Caesar's Power

Before Rome was known as an Empire, it was a Republic and, before that, a land of kings. If we were to believe the olden tales, Rome was ruled by seven kings, starting with Romulus and ending with Lucius Tarquinius Superbus. The King was a symbol of leadership and religion. At his side, 300 Senators acted as advisors, helping and guiding the King's rule, but they had no real power.

The last King of Rome was proud and cruel, and hostile methods brought upon the end of the Etruscan power. The Senate and people rose against him and expelled him from the city, thus paving the way for the republic of Rome to come about.

The republic had a slightly different government. The people elected two consuls to serve for only one year; under the consuls were the 300 senators advising them. After completing their year of service, they were forbidden from filling the position again for 10 years. During the republic, the people were divided into classes, with the upper-class ruling. There were Patricians, Plebeians, and slaves.

Patricians were the wealthy; they usually lived in luxurious homes and had slaves serving their every need. They were free citizens allowed to attend the assembly and vote. The plebeians were also citizens of Rome but of a lower class, usually traders and craftsmen. They were also allowed to vote and attend assembly.

Slaves had no rights or wealth and weren't considered citizens. Like women at the time, they weren't allowed to go to assembly or vote. During times of crises like wars, it was a custom to name a dictator until the dust settled.

The Republic of Rome marked a time of prosperity and expansion until the arrival of Caesar.

Gaius Julius Caesar was born in July 100 BC to a noble family in the republic. As a young man, he witnessed Rome fall into chaos. The wealthy hoarded riches and the average citizens struggled to get by. Slaves were revolting as their numbers increased.

Caesar possessed many talents and a sharp wit. He was funny, charming, an excellent speaker, and commanded a strong personality. He was gifted in politics and the military.

Caesar joined the army and rose in the ranks until he became a military leader. At the time, a change in purpose was introduced to the army; instead of fighting for the good of the land, they were fighting to receive land and gold. As this practice grew, the soldiers were no longer loyal to the republic but to the generals who would pay them with substantial assets. As most of the soldiers were former peasants touched by poverty and struggle, this form of compensation was more than enough for them to switch sides.

Caesar was appointed as Governor of Spain. Not only is it a prestigious position but also lucrative one. It allowed him to pillage the locals as he saw fit. Caesar forged an alliance with two other elites, General Pompey and a wealthy patrician called Crassus, thus beginning his rise to power. The three of them created the very first Triumvirate.

When he made his way back to Rome in 60 BC, he was elected consul, one of the highest offices in the republic. However, as time passed, the Triumvirate didn't survive, as Crassus was killed on the battlefield, and Pompey made his intentions known that he wished to rule by himself without the influence of Caesar.

Caesar had a huge impact on expanding the territories of Rome. While he was busy fighting for his country in Gaul (now France), The Senate, after being influenced by Pompey, decreed that he was to return home without the protection of his army after handing them over to the new governor. They also prohibited him from running for the second consulate. These actions were made in an effort to quench Caesar's rising power.

Julius Caesar was faced with two choices: either comply with the Senate's commands and return home alone, risking his reputation and maybe his life, or start a civil war. He chose the latter. Roman law decreed that no governor was allowed to cross the Rubicon back home without being invited by the Senate. The governors were only allowed to command their armies within their assigned provinces. If the law is broken, the governor and the soldiers following him would be sentenced to death after he is stripped of his imperium.

Caesar uttered his famous words, "Alea iacta est!" meaning the dice is cast, and crossed the Rubicon with his army, ushering the start of the civil war in January of 49 BC. By 46 BC, Caesar had managed to defeat the forces of Pompey and seized Rome, declaring himself a dictator and absolute ruler. He swiftly dispatched Pompey and part of the Senate out of Rome while offering amnesties to others.

Caesar went on to reform the government. He increased the size of the Senate for better representation. He offered citizenship to many foreigners, offered veterans places to settle in new cities, and was quite charitable with some of his old foes like Marcus Junius Brutus, one of Pompey's old supporters.

7. Caesar's Gallic Wars: Conquest and Triumph

Caesar knew that in order to achieve eternal glory, one must achieve unparalleled victory in battle. The Gallic campaign is one of the most remembered political and military triumphs in Caesar's long string of victories. Caesar himself wrote down an extensive record of the Great War, though it may be wise to read the scripture with a grain of salt as it was mainly written to garner political prestige for the Roman leader.

The book he wrote included seven parts, and each part was dedicated to a year of the war.

As Caesar neared the end of his Consul in 59 BC, he was gravely compromised financially. With the help of the first Triumvirate, he managed to land the position of Governor for Cisalpine Gaul and Illyricum. Following the death of the Governor of Transalpine Gaul, he was also appointed as Governor of that province.

Following his second appointment, Caesar was approached by the Helventian tribe, a Gallic tribal confederation. The delegates wished to negotiate safe passage through the Transalpine Gaul and the land of a Roman tribe called Aedui. That migration threatened chaos in the Gual area, specifically from German warrior-like tribes that may choose to occupy the vacant Helventian territory. The Roman leader denied them passage, so they changed their route away from Roman lands entirely. To the eyes of an average beholder, this seems like a situation that has resolved itself, but alas, Caesar had other plans. He saw an opportunity to defeat the migrating tribe that would alleviate his political stature and pay off his debts from the spoils.

He gathered a sum of 24000-30000 soldiers under his command and marched in pursuit of the Helventians. He managed to catch up with them as they attempted to cross the Saone River. About a quarter were unfortunate enough not to have crossed yet because Caesar slayed them all. Negotiations resumed but were futile as Caesar's terms were steep. The fighting continued until the Romans emerged victorious, and the Helventians were ordered back to their territory, starting a seven-year-long war.

Over the seven years, Caesar suffered many losses but also had many conquests to pride himself on. He conquered the Sequani territory ruled by German tribes and the Belgae confederation. He survived an ambush from the Belgic Nervii, Atrebates, and Viromandui. Attacked and conquered Gallic tribes along the English Channel. He managed to Defeat the Venti in a memorable naval battle. Caesar had no issue with mercilessly slaughtering Germanic refugees, much to Rome's Dismay. He burned down and leveled abandoned German villages. He attempted to capture Britannia but was forced back with fierce resistance from the English. He lost some of his troops to a Belgic tribe in the northeast of the Gaul led by the Eburones, to which Caesar retaliated by slaughtering the Belgic tribes.

These events ignited the Great Gallic Revolt in 52 BC. The leadership of the revolt was in the hands of Vercingetorix following the slaughter of Romans at the hands of the Carnutes. Caesar laid siege to the city of Avaricum, where he faced off against Vercingetorix, eventually entering the city after 25 days and killing all but 800 of the original 40,000 inhabitants.

Caesar eventually managed to corner Vercingetorix in the city of Alesia, where the latter's attempts to gather reinforcements failed. He was forced to surrender to the Roman leader and later was taken to Rome to be executed in 46 BC, marking the triumphant end of the Gallic wars in favor of Rome.

8. The First Triumvirate: Crassus, Pompey, and Caesar

Caesar eventually realized that to achieve glory, you might need the assistance of others. A Triumvirate is a group of three men. This word described a secret alliance forged between three individuals to grant them more power over the Roman Political entity.

The first triumvirate was forged between Gaius Julius Caesar, Gnaeus Pompeius Magnus Aka Pompey, and Marcus Licinius Crassus in 60 BC. The alliance was forged to serve the individual ambitions of each of the men. However, it was not a match made in heaven. Two of the men, Pompey and Crassus, did not get along. This was because Pompey blatantly tried and succeeded in claiming the glory of Crassus's victory over Spartacus at Capua. Sharing the praise of his hard work did not sit well with Crassus, given that the former's contribution to the victory can be summed up in him rounding up the stragglers.

As for the relationship between Pompey and Caesar, it was a little bit more amicable. Both men favored the side of the Senate that favored the Populares in the Senate (common people) and opposed the Optimates, who only cared about maintaining their power within the wealthy elites of Rome as the traditional ruling class.

Each of the leaders had his own reasons for forming this alliance. Pompey wished to reward his veteran soldiers with land in the east but was constantly opposed by Marcus

Porcius. Caesar wished to be appointed consul and reach political glory, and Crassus wished to achieve glory on the battlefield and make up for the lost funds he suffered due to the food calamity that occurred in the East.

The three men sealed their alliance by first reconciling Crassus and Pompey. To strengthen their bond further, Pompey took Caesar's daughter, Julia, for his wife.

The alliance was successful in most of its endeavors. By 59 BC, Caesar had been named co-consul with Marcus Calpurnius Bibulus, a friend of Cato. He worked hard to get Pompey the land he needed for his soldiers but was constantly vetoed by Bibulus. He then decided to take the matter into his own hands and present the proposal to the public assembly. Bibulus tried to interrupt the presentation but was thrown down the Forum steps instead and showered with garbage. Bibulus retreated from any further public appearances, which led Caesar to rule as a consul alone and grant Pompey the lands he desired. Crassus was given the chance to lead an army to cement his name as a great military leader. Unfortunately, he never achieved his dream, as he was defeated at the battle of Carrhae and decapitated by the Parthians.

9. Cleopatra and Caesar: A Fateful Alliance

Caesar first came to know Cleopatra when he pursued Pompey out of Rome in 48 BC. Pompey had first fled to Greece to assemble an army to face Caesar, succeeding in gathering twice the number of soldiers Caesar had, but it was to no avail. He was still defeated in the battle of Pharsalus. He then fled to Egypt, where Caesar followed, and that's when he was enchanted by the beautiful Queen in Alexandria, both politically and emotionally. The dispute between Queen Cleopatra and her husband/brother, Ptolemy XII, disturbed the city. Ptolemy had mistakenly assumed that killing Pompey and presenting Caesar with his head would earn his favor. He was sorely mistaken. Caesar was repulsed with the gift and, as a result, seized control of the royal palace and acted as the monarch of Egypt. He commanded the royal brother and sister to disperse their armies and to

Caesar came to know Cleopatra when he was pursuing Pompey out of Rome.[4]

settle the matter of the rightful ruler with him as their judge.

Cleopatra went to meet Caesar concealed in a carpet, as her brother's forces had blocked her from entering Alexandria. Her dramatic reveal had a much better impact on Caesar than his first meeting with her brother.

Their alliance was not built on romance and love alone; it had political aspects ingrained in it. Caesar needed Cleopatra's wealth to fund his campaign to power in Rome, and she needed his protection to secure her position as queen. His decision to declare the two siblings co-rulers again did not sit well with Ptolemy, who attempted to trap his sister with the Roman leader in the palace.

This act started a full-scale civil war in which Ptolemy was defeated in the battle of the Nile and later drowned in its namesake. Cleopatra was made Queen, and her other younger brother, Ptolemy XIV, will rule beside her. He also became her new husband despite her affair with Caesar.

Cleopatra gave birth to their son Caesarion (meaning little Caesar) shortly after. She visited Caesar in Rome a year later and stayed in one of his estates. When he was assassinated in 44 BC, she returned to Egypt, starting the tale of another affair with another Roman leader, Marc Anthony.

10. The Roman Calendar: Julius Caesar's Timeless Reform

The original dating system employed in the Republic of Rome resembled the one used in Greece, which followed the lunar cycle. It consisted of 10 months and 304 days, resulting in a 61-day gap in the winter season. In addition to continuously falling out of phase with the seasons and constantly needing correction, this lunar calendar was often exploited by the Roman officials in charge of it. They often added days to manipulate elections or extend certain political terms, abusing their authority.

In 46 BC, Caesar went to work in devising the solar calendar. He recruited Sosigenes, an astronomer from Alexandria, to aid him. Based on the solar calendar, Sosigenes calculated the year as the Egyptians do to be 365 days and a ¼. Caesar then added the missing 61 days to 46 BC, essentially moving the start of the year from March first to January first. The Julian calendar stated that the year was to be 365 days for three years in a row, followed by a year made up of 366 days (leap year). Caesar decreed that the additional day be added to February to ensure the calendar did not fall out of phase like its lunar counterpart.

Following Caesar's death, Mark Anthony renamed the month Quintilis, the 7th month of the year, to Julius (July) in honor of the fallen dictator.

11. Ides of March: Betrayal and Assassination of Julius Caesar

In Roman culture, the word Ides meant observing the full moon, which marked the 15th day and half point of every month of the Julian calendar. However, The Ides of March is a day marked in history with shame and change. By 44 BC, Caesar had appointed himself "Dictator for Life," a title that did not sit well with the powerful elite of Rome. It is argued that Caesar had sealed his fate by declaring himself as such, as Rome was known throughout history for its fight against tyrants and absolute rulers.

The conspirators behind the death of Caesar, who called themselves "The Liberators," were hung on the idea of restoring the Republic of Rome to ensure political stability.

They strongly believed that they were ridding Rome of an overly powerful tyrant. Caesar's callous ways and harsh tactics angered the aristocrats, leading them to devise a meticulous plan to end his reign.

The assassination took place in the debating chambers of the theater of Pompey, only two months after Caesar's victory over Pompey in the battle of Pharsalus.

It is believed that between 50 and 60 senators charged Caesar and stabbed him 23 times, including the two ring leaders Brutus and Cassius, whom he had considered dear companions regardless of their past allegiances with Pompey.

Cassius was unsettled by Caesar's disregard for the republican traditions and convinced Brutus, who was proud of his aristocratic heritage, to take down Caesar. Brutus held a special place in Caesar's heart as he had taken his mother, Sevilia, as a lover and considered Brutus a surrogate son. Heartbroken from the betrayal, it was said that Caesar's last famous words were "Et tu, Brute?" (You too, Brutus?). There is no way of knowing the exact words he uttered. Only those present during the betrayal could've known for sure.

Since he was stabbed so many times, it was hard to accuse any one specific person of the murder.

What the conspirators didn't see coming, though, is that following the murder of Caesar, they sealed the fate of Rome as an empire, as Caesar's adopted son Octavian later rose to power and was named Emperor Augustus.

Chapter 3: Stories of How Christianity Spread

No story of Christianity could begin without the one depicting the birth, life, and teachings of Jesus. Born in Bethlehem in Judea, Jesus belonged to the lineage of King David. The Holy Spirit aided his mother, Mary, in his conception. Mary, a young unmarried virgin, traveled with Joseph, her betrothed, to Bethlehem when they were (like many others in the region) summoned to be counted in the census. However, when they arrived, they didn't find lodging at the local inn – and were forced to spend the night in a stable. The night baby Jesus was born attracted wise men (sometimes depicted as kings, astrologers, or shepherds) who wanted to witness the product of the miraculous birth. Little is known of Jesus's childhood, but he was baptized at around 30 years old by John the Baptist.

The story of Christianity begins with the birth of Jesus.[5]

It was a time of extreme religious expectations mixed with political turmoil, prompting numerous Jewish movements to be on the lookout for the prophesized Messiah who would bring much-needed changes. John the Baptist belonged to one of these movements. He was known for spreading a message of radical transformation through repentance while baptizing locals in the Jordan River. Like John, Jesus also strived to teach and preach similar agendas from an early age. When he was baptized, he took a public ministry to spread his teachings, heal and dispel demons from the possessed, and, according to some records, bring people back from the dead. Soon, he began to travel throughout Galilee, accompanied by former fishermen who followed him with their families, deserting their nets to help spread his teachings. His message emphasized the importance of turning to God and spoke about how repentance, forgiveness, love, generosity, and justice can bring one closer to the Creator. In one of his lessons, he speaks about a man who was robbed and helped by an outsider while community members left him to his luck. Having encountered many people of different backgrounds during his ministry, Jesus warned against casting judgment and counseled critics to remember their own imperfections before condemning others (referring to what is known as the commandment to love one's neighbor).

Describing it as a unique reign of justice, Jesus claimed that the Kingdom of God is closer than people think, promising liberation for the oppressed once they repent and embrace those around them. He said that the first divine Kingdom would not be built by the wealthy, powerful rulers and distinguished members of society (as is the case with earthly kingdoms) but by societal outcasts, the rejected, and the poorest. Those who heard him began to speak of Jesus as the long-promised Messiah, the redeemer of souls. They believed he was who was prophesized to turn the Kingdom of God into a reality – marking the beginning of this new faith known as Christianity. Beginning with the followers of Jesus, Christianity spread throughout the Middle East, quickly taking over the Mediterranean coast and becoming deeply ingrained in the Roman Empire.

Initially, propagators faced vicious Roman persecutions. However, despite these, due to the appealing nature of the teachings about the spirit's immortality (living after death in the Kingdom of God), Christianity grew incredibly fast. The lessons about helping the poor also contributed to the popularization of this new religion. The Apostle Paul was one of the most prominent figures to spread Christianity in Europe (and other parts of the world). During his ministry, Paul took several missionary journeys to help those in need and spread the religion among them. Paul took at least three long missionary journeys across modern-day Syria, Turkey, Greece, Cyprus, the Roman territory of Pamphylia, and others. During his travels, he disseminated Jesus' teachings and performed miracles, laying the foundations for the early Christian church.

12. Constantine the Great: The First Christian Emperor

Emperor Constantine paved the way for Rome to become a Christian empire. Born a pagan, Constantine was baptized in 312, just before launching a war campaign against his rival, Maxentius. Worried about the outcome of the war, he asked for divine guidance. Constantine received a vision in the dream about the Christian God commanding him to use a Christian symbol on his warrior's shields. Constantine obliged and overpowered Maxentius. From then on, the emperor started to express his preference for the new religion, asking his subjects to convert and providing continuous monetary support to the Christian churches. Despite this, he also continued to give money to support traditional religion. He allowed the followers of the pagan religion to build new temples and permitted sacrifices when public buildings were destroyed by lightning – although he advocated against the practice on other occasions. It was an untraditional approach (especially in the eyes of cultures that followed a monotheistic religion). Yet, by not obligating all subjects to become fixated on worship and Christian identity, Constantine ensured his good name and wasn't at risk of being overthrown (as it happened to other rules that tried to impose Christianity). Being raised in Paganism himself, Constantine found it challenging to leave the ancient religion behind. During Constantine's rule, pagans could worship as many divine figures as they wanted and in whatever form they wished. Whether this included Jesus was up to them. Some prayed to Jesus just as they did to their other gods. After he died in 337, Constantine's three sons (all raised with the Christian faith) began to use the power of the state against the followers of the pagan religion. Constantius II, for example, banned sacrifices, closed some pagan temples, and allowed bishops to convert others into Christian churches. Even with these efforts to encourage Christianity in public life, due to the vast amount of infrastructure and the unwillingness of his administrators to enforce the anti-pagan laws, Constantius couldn't extinguish paganism.

13. From Pagan to Christian: The Transformation of the Roman Empire

While missionaries like Apostle Paul and even Constantine did their best to spread Christianity in Rome, commoners had an even more considerable influence in popularizing the religion.

Libanius, a teacher from the 4th century Rome, explains that Roman pagans didn't have a unified structure, sacred books, or rituals. He says people didn't even agree on which pagan deities were authentic. In some territories across the empire, pagans worshipped gods they imagined in human form. Whereas others saw their deities as animals or inanimate objects like giant stones. Around this time, the Roman Empire had over a million structures devoted to these pagan deities. However, the gods weren't only present here. They were incorporated into people's day-to-day lives. They were honored on holidays, and their images adorned the Roman coins. Animals sacrificed at the temples were used for the city's meat supply.

The empire already had a mighty military and civilian administration system extending across the other territories under Roman control. The Roman citizens paid taxes to the state and were given services and protection in return. They had an incredibly efficient and dynamic administrative system coupled with a highly responsive legal institution. This required drawing upon the skills and abilities of as many citizens as possible. By the 4th century, the imperial government began to identify and draw into service the young Romans living in the provincial cities and small towns. Rosters of students were given executive positions and abundant salaries. This allowed them to obtain wealth and power provided by the imperial administrative system. Born in a small town in southern France, Libanius was among the first raised and educated to take on an administrative position. His parents supported him and saw the opportunity to make the family's name and fortune larger through him. However, the young pagan men were expected to excel and work by the emperor's rules. When they got to reap the rewards of their work, Libanius and his friends used their free time to honor their traditional religion by worshipping in the surviving pagan monuments and celebrating the old festivals. At that time, the ruler was Constantine's son, Constantius II, who didn't tolerate opposition to his regime. While Libanius and others were scared of losing the remaining of their religion, they were more afraid of endangering the wealth and prominence they'd already acquired to speak out publicly. However, this all changed when Constantius died and was superseded by his cousin Julian, a publicly declared pagan.

Due to the sudden vigorous critiques of the injustice and religious fanaticism dominating his realm, Julian made plans for a pagan restoration of the empire. Although he died soon after, his Christian successors didn't focus on the Christianization of the empire, so Libanius and other pagans could continue their ways. They praised the Christian administrative system in public, lamented the autocratic tendencies in private, and continued to collect their salaries. In other words, they continued to draw parallels and talk about both religions.

Another huge shift happened in 379 when Theodosius came to power. The new ruler frantically embraced the idea of leading Rome to a new Christian era by completely eradicating pagan practices. After restricting pagan activities, he made sacrifices punishable by death, closed pagan temples, and started punishing imperial officials who neglected to enforce his laws. This made people fearful and resulted in mass conversion. The youngest Romans born in the Theodosius-ruled Rome were all Christians. The emperor ensured that people eagerly talked about Christianity, enabling him to accelerate the rate of Christianization. Spreading Christianity through word of mouth was much more effective than using the slow administrative system.

Slowly but surely, people became disinterested in pagan worship. As a result, the buildings decayed, and the number of places of worship decreased steadily. While the statues of the pagan deities remained in public places, people started to pray to the old gods and goddesses less and less. At the beginning of the 5th century, the restrictions on pagans increased even more. Even more pagan temples were closed – until there weren't enough open to bother with efforts to shut them down. While devoted pagans traveled to rural areas, they tried to enforce their own pagan views on locals, and this didn't go well. The locals were more willing to convert to Christianity than embrace different forms of Paganism.

14. Christianity and the Rise of the Medieval Church

As one would imagine, the journey of establishing the roots of Christianity in medieval Europe wasn't smooth sailing – and not just because of the pagan resistance from barbaric countries. Around the 4th century, propagators also had to compete with a new branch of Christianity, Ariasnim. Its founder was Arius, a Roman scholar whose beliefs and teachings painted a somewhat different picture than Jesus'. Followers (which included the ranks of several Roman Emperors) of Arianism spend their days acclaiming that Jesus isn't equal to God – a notion they found much more appealing than the original version. As soon as they heard this, Germanic tribes such as the Vandals, Ostrogoths, and Visigoths adopted Arisism as well, which further complicated the expansion of the original branch throughout North Africa, the Iberian Peninsula, and Italy. Some of these tribes faced heavy persecution from the Christians.

Difficulties notwithstanding, the rise of the Medieval Church was inevitable. Soon after the earliest conquers over pagans, Arians, and alike, the Bishop of Rome was proclaimed the head of the Christian church. Although initially, not all followers accepted this event (or only embraced it partially), it marked the foundations of the Papacy and its rule over the Christian church. Once, a Roman commoner was asked what they were taught about these changes. Unfortunately, they didn't know how – or what – to answer. They only knew that the Pope (as the Bishop of Rome was known across the empire) had considerable influence. They also said they were afraid of what the changes would bring because it was rumored that the Papacy was overseen and controlled by the Byzantine Empire. This was in the early medieval period. When commoners were asked the same question a couple of centuries later, they knew that the Pope's mission was to convert major parts of Western Europe and were less apprehensive about the possibility of accepting the Papacy as a supreme power. Gradually, the Roman church not only grew but separated from their co-religions in the Eastern Mediterranean. By the time the Middle Ages were in full swing, the main churches would be known as Roman Catholic and Orthodox.

15. St. Patrick and the Spread of Christianity in Ireland

St. Patrick is a well-known figure in European history and Christianity. He is credited with the religion's dissemination in Ireland and later other parts of Europe. Born in Britain in 386, St. Patrick became enslaved and sold by pirates to an Irish farm, where he spent his days working and praying. This routine shaped his mindset and even showed him the road to escape slavery. Legend has it that St. Patrick had a vivid dream telling him to go to a boat that would take him home. Being a Christian man of faith, he immediately thought it was God who spoke to him and did as was told, successfully escaping to France in 408 A.D. After a short stay in France, he found his way to his family in Britain. Here, he was ordained as a bishop in 432 A.D. and tasked with spreading Christianity by Pope Celestine I.

St. Patrick is a well-known figure in European history.[6]

Soon after, St. Patrick had yet another dream. This one depicted the Irish begging him to visit Ireland and assist the newly converted Christians in the country. He saw Irish people burdened by tribal warfare, slavery, and pagan traditions. Not wanting to let down those in need, he immediately traveled to Ireland, where, besides helping Christians, he also began to introduce the religion to the Irish pagans. To fight the resistance toward the new religion, he had the ingenious idea to incorporate pagan rituals into Christian practices.

While in Ireland, St. Patrick was attacked and captured several times by the Irish pagan tribes. However, he would always surrender willingly, as he saw the opportunity to teach his faith to his capturers. Due to his deep reverence for love, forgiveness, hard work, and social grace, he often successfully converted entire pagan tribes to Christianity. This led to the infamous saying that he drove the snakes out of Ireland (referring to the pagans).

16. The Age of Conversion: Christianizing the Barbarian Kingdoms

Despite a rough start, Christian missionaries sent from both Ireland and the Papacy were able to convert numerous rulers of European countries by the 7th century. However, the barbaric kingdoms became increasingly hard to approach after the Vikings invaded and established their rule during the 8th and 10th centuries. Thankfully, they had the support of now-Christian emperors such as Charlemagne (the Carolingian emperor), who launched a series of passionate campaigns against the Germanic tribe known as the Saxons. After a three-year invasion and destruction of numerous holy sites, the Saxons surrendered and converted to Christianity. Similar to him, Norway's Olaf Tryggvason also attempted to convert his subjects. However, his attempts were far less successful, and he was overthrown. This was around the 8th century when the majority of Norse people said, "We will never abandon the ancient religion!" Some were more resistant than others. In 1000 AD, a representative of the Alĺing (the Icelandic people's general assembly), Thorgeir Thorkelsson, was given the responsibility of deciding in 1000 whether the people of Iceland would follow Christianity or the Norse religion. He spent an entire day and the following night mulling over the issue before finally settling on the conversion. Other Scandinavian countries were also fully converted by the 11th century. By contrast, it took until after the darkest period of the Middle Ages for the Sami people of Northern Scandinavia to bow down to baptism.

During the 9th century, both the Byzantine church and the Papacy targeted the Bulgarians as the next nation to bring under their jurisdiction. However, they had to contend with the Bulgarian ruler, Boris's unusual defense strategy. Since the two sides had different interests, Boris pretended to seek an alliance with both. He was patient in determining which option would best serve his own strategic goals. He eventually came to an agreement with the Byzantine Empire, leading to the establishment of the national

Bulgarian church. The astute Bulgarians created the formal liturgy for their church using their own language and beliefs. Only a century later, Mieszko I, the first ruler of the neighboring Poland, embraced Christianity. According to legend, he was pressured into baptism by his wife, who was of Bohemian origins. I went to Boleslav I, Duke of Bohemia, Mieszko's wife's father, who was already a Christian, and asked for his loyalty. His wife told him that her father would probably support him if he converted. During the same period, the Byzantine Empire attempted to evangelize populations in other Eastern European regions, including what is now Russia and Ukraine. It was just as lagging here as it was in Scandinavia to convert. Christianity didn't become a generally accepted religion in the area until Vladimir the Great, the ruler of Kievan Rus, at the turn of the millennium. Vladimir convened with adherents of many faiths in 986, including Jews, Muslims, and Christians, before selecting his own religion to enforce upon his subjects. After learning about the culture in Constantinople (the capital of the Byzantine Empire), Vladimir and his family were baptized and embraced the teachings of the Orthodox Church.

The Hungarian ruler, King Stephen I, also embraced Christianity at the beginning of the 11th century. While initially resistant, his people followed his example of getting baptized and leaving their pagan religion behind. This took considerable effort, but everyone became more agreeable to the new faith once things were on their way. They praised Stephen I for building churches and were ready to conflict punishment on those who didn't follow Christian practices.

Being the last crucial holdouts to Christianity in Europe, the Baltic region was only fully conquered in the 14 century. This marked the end of the crusade that started in the mid-12th century and was plagued by the darkest period of the Middle Ages. The unconquered Grand Duchy of Lithuania was still a crucial regional power in the mid-14th century. However, at the end of the century, the ruling Grand Duke married the Polish Queen and was baptized as a Roman Catholic Christian based on his wife's wishes. A year later, he imposed Christianity on the Lithuanian people, although elements of their pagan faith survived past this period.

Chapter 4: Viking Expeditions and Their Stories

Originating from Scandinavia, the Vikings were mysterious Norsemen who, through their many expeditions across Europe from 750-1050 C.E., had a monumental impact on the continent's history. The Vikings were known for their exceptional sailing and navigational skills, which allowed them to travel, explore, and conquer sight far from their homeland. It's still unclear what prompted them to undertake their journeys. Historians suggest population pressure, trade, and the pursuit of wealth and prestige. This chapter explores how their journeys affected the cultures they met with and the lasting influence of Viking expeditions on European history.

The Vikings were known for their exceptional sailing and navigational skills.[7]

17. Trade and Raids: The Dual Face of Viking Expeditions

At first, Vikings thrived in their agricultural and rural society, with most clan members working as farmers and fishermen. While the fishermen would always return home with full nets, the farmers were more and more often left without a good harvest. Due to the harsh climate conditions in Scandinavia, the soil wasn't overly fertile. As their population expanded, after a while, there wasn't enough grain to keep everyone fed during the long and icy winters. As food shortages became a regular occurrence, some chieftains decided to take what their tribe needed from other tribes, marking the beginning of the Viking raids. At first, the attacks only occurred across local territories, but soon enough, they began to spread across Europe, too. As they started to expand their horizons, the Vikings found many thriving cities on the coastal area of the continent, along with monasteries – which turned out to be easy targets due to their isolation and defenseless inhabitants.

When they started to venture beyond Western Europe, the Vikings slowly began settling, trading, and farming in their new homelands. Journeying across the North Atlantic and through the icy rivers to Constantinople, they reached North America at the beginning of the 11th century (over 400 years before Columbus). While their colony here was short-lived, their settlements in other parts of Europe thrived beyond imagination. Their voyages, accompanied by a reign of terror, soon became history. Some tribes, not all, even started to embrace Christianity (albeit very slowly), which meant they ceased raiding monasteries. The favorable climate outside Scandinavia also made farming more feasible, so there was no need to continue the sea-faring warrior lifestyle.

As the Vikings gradually embraced trade and settlement, they were driven by the same goals as they were during their raids. They were after wealth, even if this meant obtaining fertile agricultural land. Naturally, they had to interact with the locals, which was often a hit or miss. In England, for example, they started coming with the Britons, even embracing the hybridization of their cultures. Meanwhile, the Vikings kept to themselves in Russia and Normandy, remaining a minority – although they did their best to blend their culture and respect the locals. All across Europe, the Vikings traded weapons, tools, soap, jewelry, cooking vessels, and building materials. Wherever they started bartering, they established enormous commercial centers, reviving small, dying markets and areas – much to the local population's happiness and benefit.

18. The Sacking of Lindisfarne: The Dawn of the Viking Age

The Vikings first attacked a monastery looking for loot at Lindisfarne in 793 A.D. The Vikings' killing and enslaving of defenseless monks caused outrage – but the symbolic defeat was even more prominent. Medieval Christians considered Lindisfarne one of the birthplaces of Christianity in Britain. They viewed the sacking of this site as a desecration of the Creator's sanctuary and shedding the blood of monks akin to dispersing waste across the streets. In a letter to Higbald (the bishop of Lindisfarne at the time), a priest named Alcuin claimed that the attack was God's punishment for the monks of Lindisfarne. He was sure the lamentable event was a sign of some terrible mistake. Since he didn't know what the sin was, Alcuin advised the surviving monks to avoid drinking ale, wearing fancy clothes, and other "frivolous" behavior, pray even more often than usual, and fortify their faith in God. He also prompted the relocation of the surviving relics and artifacts (like St. Cuthbert's body) to another, less accessible location.

According to another record of the event, people saw dragons flying across the sky above Lindisfarne before the attack. The woefully terrified locals claimed to see fiery dragons sail the sky, letting out immense sheets of burning light. They even tied the great famine that soon followed to this event, along with heathen men wreaking havoc in the church of God on Holy Island (referring to the Viking raid of Lindisfarne). However, none of them could've imagined that the sacking of Lindisfarne was only the beginning of the Viking's reign of terror in Britain. Through the following years, the Vikings led entire armies into Britain, making significant conquests along the way.

19. The Vikings in Russia: The Rus' Legacy

Britain was only their first target when the Vikings started spreading from Scandinavia. As they began to head east, along the Dnieper and Volga rivers, they saw the opportunity to take control of trade routes that enabled them to reach the mighty Byzantine Empire. Lured by trade opportunities and wealth, they advanced to Constantinople. From the 9th century onwards, these Vikings spreading toward the west became known as the Rus (or Varangians). They conquered the territories of modern-day Russia, Ukraine, and Belarus. Establishing a ruling point in Kyiv in 840, they were named the Kievan Rus. According to the Russian Primary Chronicle (a historical account of the region compiled in the 12th century by Kievan monks), the rule over their territory was initially divided between three brothers. Truvor established a base in Izborsk, Sineus, at Beloozero, while the third brother, Rurik, lived at Novgorod. The latter became known as the capital of the land of the Rus (the original form of the name "Russia"). After their death, Ririk claimed his brother's territory, making Novgorod the capital of the entire domain of the Rus. His successor, Oleg, relocated the capital to Kyiv. True to his Viking ancestors, Oleg continued to conquer new territories, increasing the rule of Kievan Rus and amassing incredible wealth through lucrative trade with Constantinople.

According to legends, a prophecy foretold Oleg that he would die riding one of his horses. To avoid this, Oleg stopped riding that animal. However, after successfully expanding his territory (and thinking himself invincible), Oleg began to consider riding the horse once again — only to discover that it had died. He did, however, find its bones. Satisfied that it would never cause his demise now, Oleg stomped on the animal's skull.

Just at that moment, a snake shot from underneath the animal's bones and bit him. Oleg died soon after.

Oleg's successor was Rurik's son, Igor, who, like his predecessor, set out to conquer and trade. Unfortunately, he wasn't good at collecting bounty from the conquered territories, and the tribes rebelled against the high prices, killing him. He was succeeded by his wife Olga, who, according to the stories, took revenge on her husband's killers. When the emissaries (belonging to the tribes her husband wanted to conquer) went to see her, Olga made them believe that she would marry one of them – only to trick them into being burned alive in her bathhouse.

When Vladimir the Great assumed rule and embraced Christianity, the era of the Kievan Rus started to come to an end. Besides agreeing to convert to Christianity, Vladimir also sent the emperor of the Byzantine Empire 6,000 soldiers to defend his throne. He was allowed to marry the emperor's sister in exchange, forging a powerful alliance between the two domains. As a result of this deal, the Kievan Rus began to embrace the Byzantine culture. Vladimir erected churches to encourage people to practice the new faith, even building schools to improve literacy (adding to the spread of Christianity). While the economy flourished and Kievan Rus continued to expand, after the rule of Vladimir's son Yaroslav I, the federation fell victim to royal power struggles. Further instability was caused by the Crusades, and by the time the Mongols invaded the territory in the 13th century, the Kievan Rus stood no chance of fighting back.

20. The Viking Siege of Paris: A City Under Threat

France's (known as the Frankish Empire at the time) first encounter with Viking raiders in 799 marked the beginning of an extended period of raids of the territory. However, it wasn't the most memorable of the Viking attacks – even though the empire had plenty of time to prepare its future defense strategy. In 810, Emperor Charlemagne established an early defense system of watchtowers and coastal forts across the northern coast. To fortify its response to the threat posed by Viking raids, the defense system was backed up by a sizable establishment of a naval fleet that would patrol along the coastline. Although this didn't stop the Vikings from continuing their reign of terror across the Frankish Empire, the defense system did stop their attack at the mouth of the river Seine.

Unfortunately, two and half decades later, the defense system failed when Danish Vikings in Frisia and Dorestad broke through, commencing a systematic raid pattern in the religion. These raids had political motivations. Rather than continuing their sporadic attacks, Vikings began to plan and coordinate their strategies, leading them to more sizable bounties and minimal losses. It also involved setting up permanent bases in the conquered areas, leading to the establishment of early Viking settlements. Moreover, the raids across the Frankish Empire were often the result of power struggles among

Scandinavian Vikings. Tribe leaders wanted to expand their territories and gain more power to establish dominance over rival tribes.

The chieftains accumulated wealth and status, and the spoils were distributed among the raider warriors. Naturally, the most successful warriors got them, which led to fierce competition among the leaders. Historians theorize that this was behind the sudden shift in tactics toward more organized raiding.

As the raids grew more frequent and brutal, they caused widespread panic among the locals. When the Viking settlements started growing in number, it threatened to destabilize the Frankish Empire. The reason was simple: the newly established settlements served as excellent bases for attacks and could serve as bases for further Viking attacks.

Amid all this chaos, the Vikings arrived in Paris in 1845, immediately launching an attack by entering the city, pillaging, and causing destruction on their way. Led by Reginherus, thousands of Viking warriors arrived in the Seine on 120 ships, quickly powering through the Frankish defense made from a smaller army put together by King Charles in haste. Even a short-lived plague outbreak in their camp didn't stop the Vikings from plundering and occupying the city.

Charles made further attempts to push back the invasion but to no avail. When he realized he couldn't overpower the Vikings, he decided to pay them a ransom of 7,000 livres of gold and silver — asking them to withdraw their forces in return. While the substantial amount of precious metal was well received by the Vikings, they only viewed it as compensation for earlier defeats (they lost lands and settlements to Charles's army earlier). More payments followed in an attempt to buy time and make peace with the Vikings in the future. The payments are known as Danegeld, although it's unclear whether this term was used at the time. Charles was heavily criticized for paying the ransom, but he also had to deal with local revolts across his reign, pressures from other European rulers, and even disputes with his brothers. Paying off the Vikings was a prudent move to avoid further conflict and take at least one burden off the shoulders of the Frankish Empire.

While the Vikings eventually withdrew from the city, the Siege of Paris in 845 was a pivotal point in the European past. It brought forth the dangers of a clash between two very different cultures. Moreover, the Vikings forever carved their name into history by triumphing over the Franks. While the invasion wasn't a complete success, it left its mark on the entire continent, and according to some, its effect can still be felt (even if only in France). Even more importantly, the tribes continued to loot along the coast while traveling back to their home settlements. Their expansion into the empire continued, and they were able to demonstrate their military prowess many times over in the future. For the Franks, the defeat exposed their vulnerability to enemy attacks.

21. The Danelaw: Vikings in England

After the attack on Lindisfarne, The Vikings continued their raids on the country's northeast coast. They ransacked other monasteries, heralding the 300-year-long Viking age England (and the rest of Europe) was about to endure. The Vikings continued to loot on Irish, Scottish, and Irish soil in the following years. Eventually, they grew tired of moving around to raid and started conquering usable lands. The most notable invasion was led by Ivar the Boneless and Halfdan Ragnarsson (both sons of Ragnar). After amassing an immense force of the Great Heathen Army (as it was called by the famous Anglo-Saxon Chronicle), the Vikings were ready to conquer. Besides wanting to settle, Ragnar's sons were also led by revenge for their father's death. According to the Norse sagas, the King of Northumbria is said to have slain Ragnar by plunging him into a pit filled with poisonous snakes.

England was split into four kingdoms upon the arrival of the Viking army, namely Wessex, East Anglia, Mercia, and Northumbria. East Anglia's ruler quickly bargained with the Vikings to rescue himself and his followers. Therefore, the invasion didn't continue long there. In return for sparing his kingdom and subjects, the king provided the warriors with his best horses to continue their campaign. Shortly after, the Vikings conquered York, the capital of Northumbria, and the rothers were able to take their revenge on its king. In his place, they put a ruler they could manage, and they led their army forward in search of more territory.

After a decade of conflict, only the kingdom of Wessex remained unconquered. It was ruled by Alfred the Great, who, after encountering the Danish warlord and Viking leader Guthrum at the Battle of Edington, claimed a victory against the barbarians. This led to a temporary peace agreement between the Vikings and the kingdom of Wessex. Known as the Treaty of Wedmore, the consensus prompted Guthrum to embrace Christianity (and undergo baptism) and Alfred to become his godfather. Guntrum was also to withdraw his army from the kingdom. Soon after, Guthrum and Alfred came to another agreement that outlined their respective domains and trading possibilities in detail, guaranteeing a more durable peace.

Following the new agreement, Viking laws and customs extended throughout the kingdom, reaching the northern boundaries, the Midlands, and London on the southern side. The name of this region was identified as Danelaw, derived from the Old English term Dena lagu, meaning "Danes' law."

The Danelaw region.[8]

While the Vikings didn't have colonies across this entire area, they had bases in five critical points in the east. These were Lincoln, Leicester, Derby, Nottingham and Stamford. These were initially just the outposts of five Viking armies that had invaded and established themselves in the region. As they developed into towns, they were dubbed the Five Boroughs and were governed by Viking Jarls. Even though they operated separately, all of them were clearly under the direct authority of the Yorkist kings.

The Anglo-Saxons and the Vikings coexisted for many decades after that, trading, blending together, and creating mixed communities. The language and place names of the Danelaw that have persisted to this day show the most obvious effects of their coexistence. For instance, the Old Norse word for "village" was the source of the suffix -

by, frequently used at the end of Viking settlement names (like Derby, for example). Other Viking place names begin with 'sky' or 'skin.' Modern Britons even have the Vikings to thank for the words "law" and "wrong," none of which existed in Old English. They were all incorporated into English after establishing a legal system in Danelaw.

Unfortunately, peace could only last for so long. After almost a century, conflicts began to arise between the Vikings and their neighbors once again. By this time, Alfred took advantage of the peace agreements to reinforce his army and erect numerous forts for better defense against the Vikings. He was succeeded by his eldest daughter, Æthelflæd, who heroically led the fight against the barbarians. She began by taking over the rule of the kingdom of Mercia, where she found the resources she needed to launch an offensive strategy against the Vikings. This move played a significant role in Danelaw's conquest. By 954 A.D., the Five Boroughs had fallen, and Eric Bloodaxe, the most brutal Viking and current King of Northumbria, was displaced from the region. This marked the end of Danelaw in England.

Despite Danelaw's eradication in England, the Vikings were very active on English soil. While they seemingly ceased their raids and retreated to other settlements, they would return. They marched for the English cities shortly after gathering their armies, and less than a century later, they had already triumphantly taken over the nation. Sweyn Forkbeard became the first Danish king of England in 1013. Cnut the Great, his son, succeeded him until he died in 1035. The last Viking monarch, Harald Hardrada of Norway, was not vanquished until the English army under monarch Harold's command won the Battle of Stamford Bridge in 1066.

In the same way, their culture left a permanent legacy across the European continent (and beyond). Viking traditions persisted in the region of former Danelaw long after the warriors suffered their last defeat. The decades of coexistence left its trace in the local population, whose DNA is still heavily laced with Scandinavian roots.

Chapter 5: Stories of a Black Death Most Deadly

Following the sudden spread of the most recent pandemic, Covid-19, people have since started looking back on historic milestones that may resemble the heart-wrenching effects of this unfortunate outbreak. One of the most unforgettable tragedies in human history that involves pestilence is the Black Death. It's also known as the Great Mortality in reference to the highest fatality rate caused in history (historic documentation of estimated fatalities has varied significantly between 25–200 million deaths), which amounted to about a third of the population.

The behemoth that is the Black Death was a threat the European continent did not see coming prior to the 14th century. The infamous plague is guilty of reaping more lives than any war or illness has ever done before it. It is a popular belief that modern-day epidemics originated from the medieval period, making this a disease that's been passed down through generations in different forms.

The behemoth that is the Black Death was a threat to the European continent.[9]

Origins of the Black Death

The Black Death originally made its presence known in the inner parts of Asia and China. It left its footprint on the Mongol warriors of Kipchak Khan Janibeg when he attempted to lay siege to the Genoese port of Kaffa in Crimea (known today as Feodosiya) in 1347. The plague did not deter him from his quest; instead, he harnessed it as a Bioweapon using trebuchets to catapult his infected, deceased soldiers into the town of Kaffa, hoping they would infect the town's people.

As a result of Janibeg's inhumane tactics, the Black Death was carried by Genoesian ships from the Black Sea that were westbound. They delivered it to the Mediterranean ports (Messina, Italy), effectively inflicting the horrors of the pestilence on western Eurasia and North Africa for the following few years.

Giovanni Boccaccio painted a morbid picture of the Black Plague in the Decameron. He said, "A great many breathed their last in the public streets, day and night; a large number perished in their homes, and it was only by the stench of their decaying bodies that they proclaimed their death to their neighbors. Everywhere, the city was teeming with corpses."

By 1350, the Black Plague had made its way all across Europe, reaching the North, including England, Scotland, Scandinavia, and the Baltic countries.

While many historians argue that the plague was exterminated by 1353, evidence supports its recurrence several times from 1360 to 1400. It is thought to have arrived in Europe in waves from central Asia through scores of rodents affected by climate change and infested with plague-carrying fleas.

Modern researchers conclude that the disease was caused by bacillus bacteria called Yersinia Pestis. This bacterium is believed to have traveled not only on the backs of rodents but also through humans, hibernating in lice, biding their time to wreak havoc on Medieval Europe. Researchers believe that the Black Death consisted of three plagues. Bubonic, Pneumonic, and Septicemic. The one believed to have infiltrated Europe the most in the 14th century is the Bubonic Plague, with symptoms that included swelling in Lymph Nodes (specifically around the armpits and groin), creating sores that then turn into black scabs, hence the name Black Plague. It also caused a running fever and joint pain. This type was often responsible for 30–75% of deaths of the total people afflicted by it if it was left untreated within the first 72 hours. You might think this type of plague is catastrophic; however, the other two types – Pneumonic and Septicemic plagues — were fatal to all infected.

The Black Death's Impact

While the physical damage this disease caused to the population at the time was cataclysmic, it had other unpleasant effects that reshaped the continent for quite some time. This disease left its fingerprints on the economy, religious institutions, politics, and societal conditions. Each of these stories depicts the cruelty of some humans when faced with traumatic events.

22. Flagellants and Fanatics: Religious Responses to the Black Death

When people were first privy to the Black Death, they treated their dead with as much respect as ever. The mourners would assemble coffins and go through the traditional burial rituals of their loved ones. However, as it became clear that this disease was more vicious than anyone had ever thought and was here to stay for a while, people grew desperate, and the officials declared that the dead would be buried in mass graves due to the huge number of corpses, and lack of space for singular plots.

Due to a shortage of land, Pope Clement VI went as far as consecrating the Rhone River so they could get rid of the corpses in it.

The peasants who witnessed the calamity that was happening were mortified. They believed that the plague was a result of the wrath of God. Their beliefs were backed by the declaration from the Roman Catholic Church, which also asserted this belief. They beseeched the citizens to pray and made a point of organizing religious marches to ask God to spare them from the disease. Nonetheless, even through all of these religious efforts, doubts started seeping through people's minds as they saw their religious figures (Monks, Nuns, and Friars) dying as easily as the rest of them. In some places, the religious services and sermons stopped because no one was around to lead them.

People started to find refuge in magic, protective talismans, and spells. Others burned incense, thinking that the stench of the dead was the reason for the illness. Many more thought they could chase the disease away with cannon fire and church bells.

These unfortunate circumstances paved the way for the birth of the Flagellant Movement. The movement consisted of a group of penitents that traveled together from one place to another while whipping themselves in an effort to atone for their sins. These motions originated in Austria and later picked up momentum in Germany and France. Those fanatics, who were often led by self-proclaimed masters with no religious credibility whatsoever, had a major hand in spreading the plague further. They also caused havoc in societies when they made it a habit to attack minorities like the Jews. The faith in the church started to diminish as a direct result of the scandals and the shameful conduct and thriftless attitude of clergy, leading people to believe that the plague was a result of the paranormal.

23. Scapegoats in Crisis: Persecution of Jews During the Black Death

Fear was the strongest catalyst of this prejudice and aggression. One of the most unfortunate consequences of the Black Plague was the containment of Jewish society.

Christian believers attributed the disease to Jewish magic, believing that the Jews had deliberately poisoned the wells to harm the Christians using black magic. As more people lost faith in the church and started to look for supernatural explanations, many directed that unneeded attention to the Jewish community, including the fanatics of the Flagellant Movement.

Some Jews were coerced into confessing through torture, and later, around 20 Jews were murdered. King Peter of Aragon made an effort to dial down the hostilities against the Jewish community; however, that didn't stop the riots that broke out across Europe against them, forcing several monarchs to issue orders for their arrest.

This mania spread like wildfire to communities that hadn't yet been touched by the plague. In Chillon, not far from Geneva, the Jews were attacked four months before any of the locals fell ill. This was triggered by the well-poisoning rumor that spread from afflicted areas.

A lot of the crimes committed against the Jews happened in areas that spoke mainly German; however, it is thought to have originated in French and Spanish territories. Some historians argue that there was no direct relation between the massacres and the occurrence of the disease, while others claim that the burning of Jews started before the disease made its way to Europe. In other tales, the Christian governments were to blame for what was believed to be a meticulous plan executed to target the Jews.

There were two prevailing theories to explain the injustice the Jews suffered from. The scapegoating effect and the complementariness effect. The scapegoating effect was a result of the downward slope the illness was taking, leading people to blame the marginalized group in society for it (not unlike how Asians were targeted and blamed for Covid-19 in 2020). The complementary effect was due to the huge impact the Jews had on the economy, making the roles they filled more integral as the Plague hit.

Anti-Semitism spread almost as fast as the Plague by the wealthy and powerful who were indebted to the Jews (later referred to as Jew Killers) in an effort to absolve themselves of their debts.

At the start of the Black Death, it was estimated that Jewish communities were present in around 363 cities. By the end of the Pestilence, it is believed that almost half of these communities were either exterminated or forced to leave their homes.

24. Social Upheaval: The Peasants' Revolt and the Plague

The Black Plague significantly impacted the social status quo, taking Medieval Europe by storm. In England, a significant shortage of laborers and peasants occurred, and an estimated 40% of its population perished from the Plague (the height of such loss was between the summer of 1348 and the spring of 1350). Being an agricultural nation that depended on the abundance of lower-class workers at the time, this caused quite a crisis, specifically for the upper-class citizens of the society. When the workers realized a higher demand for their skills, they started to bargain with their masters for better wages. They abandoned their villages in search of higher pay in exchange for their services. These acts caused a great deal of dismay among the upper classes, who, until the Plague had hit, enjoyed luxuries and privileges that the peasants only witnessed from afar.

After a lot of pressure from the lords of the lands on the government, the statute of laborers was passed with the blessing of King Edward III.

The law entailed that the peasants and workers were not to take advantage of the shortage of laborers and ask for extra wages but were forced to work in exchange for the same wages they had accepted before the Black Plague. These wages were to be determined by the people who hired them. A new tax poll was forced on all peasants (men and women) regardless of their wealth.

This caused an uproar in the lower classes not only because it limited their income but because of the events that followed.

People who tried to flee their homes seeking better pay were dragged back by force by the landlords. Any workers who refused to abide by the law would expect physical penalties and hefty fines from the local lords. Some of the landowners tried to turn people into serfs or villeins (old-fashioned tenants who paid their dues to the landlords through service in return for land) to save money by not paying wages.

These evil and unjust acts were the fuel that lit the peasant revolt, also known as the great revolt. The lower class endured for 30 years following the law's decree until they marched from their villages to London in May of 1381. The Christian values that all men are born equal and should be treated with respect were used by the revolters to back up the campaign. On the other hand, the institution of the Medieval Church was condemned for many of the society's shortcomings.

The commoners rose against the old shackles that entailed that people who were born in privilege were above them and deserved more. A chant was repeated: "When Adam delved and Eve span, who then was the gentleman." It expressed their rage at being treated with inequality. They burned down buildings and set prisoners free. Sheriffs and officials were taken and killed. Manors were torched, burning most of the records at Maidstone, Canterbury, and Rochester in an effort to destroy the seignorialism.

As the villagers arrived in London on June 13th, they were met with more disgruntled commoners who had their own feuds with the rich in the city. A lot of the lawyers and crown officials were targeted as a result of old grievances and grudges. On June 14th, King Richard II, believed to have only been 14 at the time, left the safety of the London Tower to meet with the peasants and hear their demands at Mile End. The King listened to the demands recited to him by the leader of the peasants, Wat Tyler of Maidstone (he was believed to have been accompanied by another leader, the demagogue Priest John

Ball). Richard agreed to the demands and even allowed the peasants to exact vengeance on whomever they thought deserved it.

Following this meeting, the London Tower was stormed, and the Archbishop of Canterbury, Simon Sudbury, was captured and executed by a mob led by Johanna Ferrour.

The looting and murder continued for another day, causing the King to call for another meeting with the rebel's leader on June 15th, this time in a field in Smithfield outside of London. The demands made in this meeting included:

- The complete abolition of Serfdom and villeins
- All to receive free fishing and hunting rights
- A retraction of the labor law that limited increases in wages
- The church riches are to be redistributed, specifically that of great abbeys
- The participation of peasants in the government
- The only authority should be in the hands of the crown and not delegated to the landlords

The remainder of the meeting is shrouded in mystery. Some say that Tyler was agitated and seemed to have intended to strike the King; some say he spat water at the King's feet. As a result, either William Walworth, the Mayor of London, or a soldier of the King's guard stepped up and stabbed him. It is said that he fled the meeting and managed to be taken to a hospital for treatment, only to be brought back to Smithfield to be executed. The King declared to the crowd that their demands shall be met. He stated that he is their leader and that they should go home as they have fulfilled their quest. Many peasants heeded his words and returned to their lands; however, the King did not intend to keep his word.

Instead of honoring his promise, King Richard went out of his way to round up almost 150 of the rebels and execute them by hanging. There were smaller attempts for rebellion after that, which were ruthlessly annihilated, and their ring leaders executed as traitors, including John Ball, who wasn't only hanged but dismembered as well.

Tyler's head was put on display on the London Bridge.

As disappointing as this outcome was, following the King's short imprisonment and unexplained death, some reforms started to blossom in England. The poll tax was revoked, and the limitations placed on wages were not as strictly enforced, while villains could buy their freedom from their landlords. The laws no longer served to condemn the peasants to servitude but to document that the laborer had indeed bought their freedom and that the land was theirs to pass down to their lineage.

25. A Blow to Feudalism: Economic Impacts of the Black Death

Not unlike what we're experiencing today in the aftermath of Covid-19, the economy following the spread of the Black Plague was extremely inflated. The disease made it difficult and unsafe to acquire or manufacture products due to quarantine and fear of infection, so the prices for local and foreign goods went through the roof. Many households who have lost their breadwinners were dependent on charities to sustain them, which put a strain on the civic entities of the governments.

While the peasants' revolt did not conclude in a positive resolution for the economic status of the lower class, in the long run, things seemed to look up a bit. With the gradual fading of serfs, workers no longer had to man any one land, and they were free to roam and find better compensation for their work, reshaping the face of the agrarian economy. Due to the scarcity of workers following the death toll of the Black Death, if one were to leave a lord, another would hire them immediately. The standards of living were ultimately raised all around. Per capita incomes and wages started to grow. With the increase of wealth for the lower class came the ability to buy more products, which increased the production of the demanded goods. The economic position of Europe following the plague was altered drastically in comparison to other continents like Asia.

26. Surviving the Plague: Stories of Resistance and Resilience

The stories of the Black Death are not all tales of despair and societal melancholy. Some stories inspire resilience, recovery, and courage in facing the unknown. Look at the cultural response to the Pestilence's arrival in Europe. You'll notice that it varied between finding purpose in the face of horrific circumstances through spiritual enlightenment and salvation in the afterlife or through fighting for justice and liberation. These themes were heavily emphasized in the 14th century.

Evidence of resilience can be found in artistic expressions observed in literature like The Decameron, written by Giovanni Boccaccio, or The Canterbury Tales by Geoffrey Chaucer, inspired during the Plague. It also affected the art world as a wide collection of paintings was produced during the Black Death.

Now, it is true that the Plague had a deadly immediate touch on the economy. In hindsight, though, the way communities seemed to bounce back, pick up the pieces, and reassemble the societal structure in a better and just manner is proof of how the people afflicted by the tragedy adapted to the changes promptly and efficiently.

One of the most debated theories in history is the "light touch" of the Plague in the southern areas of Europe. This story mainly focuses on the southern Netherlands, which was deemed fictitious. It suggested that the lower countries were not as affected by the Black Death as the rest of Europe; however, it does shed light on the ease with which these areas managed to recover their population. As it turns out, some believe that this was due to the resilient urban settlements allowing migrants from devastated rural areas to take refuge in their lands.

Chapter 6: Renaissance Stories

The Renaissance is a pivotal era in European history that is characterized by the rise of distinguished families who transformed the cultural and political landscape of the region. This chapter explores the tales of influential families that shaped the Italian Renaissance. You will learn about their political, cultural, and economic power and influence.

The Renaissance is a pivotal era in European history that is characterized by the rise of the cultural and political landscape.[10]

Italy was organized into several city-states, such as Siena, Florence, Venice, and Naples, at the time the Medicis rose to power. The Medicis attained power in Florence in 1434, where the Renaissance started, and ruled for over six decades. Wealthy families in this affluent, cultural place could afford to support rising artists, a movement the Medici family supported.

The Medici are among the most influential families in European history. They established Florence as a cultural hub, transformed the banking industry, made political reforms, and were patrons of the arts, giving rise to the High Renaissance, which was a period of flourishing artistic endeavors.

27. Advancements in Banking and Finance

Cosimo the Elder built the Medici bank in Florence, which later branched across other city-states and even foreign cities like Bruges and London. The branches he opened in the neighboring countries allowed the Papacy to order goods from outside Italy.

The strategic locations of the branches, alongside their invention of transformative financial tools, made them pioneers in the banking industry. For instance, they introduced the double-entry bookkeeping system, now considered a basic and fundamental finance and accounting principle. Transcontinental payments were risky at the time, which was a problem that the Medicis took care of by inventing the Letters of Credit, which serve as proof of payment yet to be received.

Patronage and Artistic Flourish

The Medici family helped establish some of the most popular Italian landmarks, including St. Peter's Basilica, the Sistine Chapel, and the Duomo of Florence, through their patronage, relationships, and political strategies. Florence didn't have the strongest military force compared to other Italian city-states, making it vulnerable to attacks. The fact that the Medicis were skilled diplomats significantly helped their position.

Cosimo the Elder brilliantly negotiated his way through a series of wars in Lombardy, ending them because he knew that the clash would hurt trade procedures. He was able to help all the states come to an agreement regarding mutual territory, which Lorenzo de' Medici, his successor, kept alive. Lorenzo was loved by the people because he freed slaves and performed other similar kind acts.

Some suggest that Botticelli's Pallas and the Centaur was made in honor of Lorenzo, as his negotiation skills also protected Florence and its independence against cities with strong armies. Lorenzo embodied Pallas Athena's wisdom, and Naples portrayed humanity's fertility, which is symbolized by the centaur. Lorenzo was also among the most prominent Medici art patrons, as he supported many major artists like Michelangelo and Botticelli.

Lorenzo de' Medici met Michelangelo while studying at the Academy of San Marco. Despite being a teen at the time, the artist impressed Lorenzo with his carving skills and got invited to stay at the place for two years. During his stay, Michelangelo became Donatello's student and formed lasting friendships with Lorenzo's sons, who would later become Popes Clement Vii and Leo X. The artist was later commissioned to paint the Sistine Chapel's upper walls by Pope Julius II and returned 25 years later to paint the

Last Judgment. Donatello was also commissioned to create the world-renowned bronze David and the Judith and Holofernes.

Architectural Evolution

Tuscany's first Duke, Cosimo I de' Medici, initially established the Uffizi as an administrative center for the family. However, it was transformed into a public art gallery featuring numerous remarkable artworks, including Botticelli's "The Birth of Venus" and Bandinelli's "Laocoön and his Sons."

Cosimo the Elder commissioned the Duomo of Florence, which faced numerous delays due to the technical challenges architects faced while constructing it without Gothic buttresses. However, Brunelleschi proved that he could build the dome without the scaffolding, creating one of the world's tallest structures. Pope Leo X also oversaw the construction of St. Peter's Basilica, a project that Martin Luther questioned.

The Conspiracies and Resilience That Inspired Interesting Work

In 1478, Giuliano de' Medici and Lorenzo the Magnificent were attacked during a public mass. While the former died, Lorenzo the Magnificent survived with injuries. Witnessing the assassination attempt, angry citizens captured and killed the conspirators. The Medici family stayed in power, and the event was commemorated in art.

The Medici family was later exiled to Rome from 1494 to 1512 due to political issues and was replaced by an anti-Medici family. The statue of David, which was initially commissioned for religious purposes, was placed in the town hall. The government-oriented David's eye in Rome's direction, giving it a new political meaning.

During the Medici's exile, Machiavelli, a theorist and diplomat, networked with Anti-Medici figures. He was, therefore, placed on the Medici's list of conspirators as soon as they made it back to Florence. The philosopher was tortured and imprisoned but was eventually spared the execution on account of Pope Leo X. Machiavelli later dedicated "The Prince" to the next Medici ruler in hopes of securing a position within the court. Needless to say, his efforts failed.

Headway in the Worlds of Science, Music, and Fashion

The First Duke of Tuscany published a book about his telescope-based discoveries, which included his observation of Jupiter's moons, in 1610 after he was tutored by Galileo Galilei. The family also made musical advances, which included the financial support of significant opera houses. The piano was also invented by Bartolomeo Cristofori while he was working in the family's court.

Catherine de' Medici also made advancements in the worlds of fashion and equestrian sports. She commissioned a pair of high-heeled shoes because she wanted to appear taller, establishing the fashion statement as a symbol of wealth and status.

This was a bold move on her part because, at the time, high heels were popular among butchers who wished to avoid getting blood on their feet. The noblewoman also popularized side-saddle riding so more women could ride without feeling exposed.

The Last of the Medici

The Medici bloodline ended with Gian Gastone de' Medici, Tuscany's last Grand Duke, who had no male heirs. Anne Maria Luisa de' Medici understood that Francis of Lorraine would inherit the power in Tuscany and that all her family's property would be automatically passed on to him. She, therefore, declared that everything that belonged to her family would remain in Florence to adorn the city, benefit its people, and attract foreigners.

28. The Borgia Family: A Papacy Marred by Scandal

The Borgia family is among the Renaissance's most famous yet controversial Italian noble families. The Borgias originally came from the Spanish Kingdom of Valencia and relocated to Italy. Their rule significantly influenced the history of Italy and the Catholic Church. Despite their scandalous stories and controversies, the family supported several artists and intellectuals at the time.

The Borgias' Ascent to Power

Alfonso de Borgia pursued a degree in canon and civil law, cultivating a successful career path in the field of politics as well as being invested in the church. He was a diocese representative and worked his way up until he became King Alfonso V of Aragon's secretary and Vice-Chancellor. He then became regent when the King went to conquer Naples.

Alfonso earned Rome's recognition and became both priest and bishop when he negotiated over a rival pope. A few years later, Alfonso traveled to Naples to reorganize the government before he represented Aragon at a council to reconcile the Western and Eastern churches. Although it failed, he established himself as a masterful diplomat.

Alfonso played a crucial role that helped the King negotiate papal approval for his rule of Naples and was therefore rewarded with the title cardinal in 1444. A year later, he moved to Rome at the age of 67. Unlike the rest of his family, he was an honest, sober, and dedicated man who would later create a more scandalous reputation for the family and Rome. One of Alfonso's nephews, Rodrigo, studied canon law and ended up working for the church. Although he had an esteemed job, he was infamous for his romantic pursuits. Alfonso's other nephew became a commander in the army.

Alfonso's Rise to Papacy

In the same year he returned to Rome, Alfonso was elected Pope because he wasn't involved with any major groups, and a short reigning period was ideal for his age. Upon receiving the title, Alfonso changed his name to Calixtus III. As a Spaniard ruling in Rome, Calixtus had several enemies. He followed a cautious ruling strategy to avoid them along with the major groups in the city. However, he didn't receive a warm welcome as the people rioted into his first ceremony. He also broke away from King Alfonso V after ignoring his request to go on a crusade.

Calixtus promoted his family, naming Rodrigo and his older brother, Pedro, cardinals and securing a range of positions for other family members. Being in their mid-20s, the brothers didn't take their positions seriously and engaged in acts that scandalized the city. Rodrigo was then made papal legate in another city, a position in which he demonstrated success and talent. He later became second in command of the church. Pedro also switched positions and was granted an army command. He, too, was very skillful and eventually became promoted to Prefect and Duke.

Pedro went on a mission to conquer Naples when King Alfonso V died. Many people believe that Calixtus planned to have Pedro rule over Naples. However, Pedro had to fight with rivals over the jurisdiction of Naples and soon died of malaria. Calixtus' death followed in 1458.

Rodrigo Finally Becomes Pope

Rodrigo played a role in electing Pius II as the next pope. He knew, however, that he was in danger because he was a young Spaniard without a patron. He then decided to establish himself as a salient ally to the Pope and secured his position as Vice-Chancellor. Rodrigo was capable of proving himself worthy of the title. However, what overpowered his skill was his love for money and women. He, therefore, didn't follow in his late uncle's footsteps and was even reprimanded by the Pope for his inappropriate conduct and romantic affairs. Instead of taking it as a serious warning and focusing more on his career, Rodrigo tried to become more discreet. Regardless of his cautiousness, Rodrigo ended up with many children. Cesare, born in 1475, and Lucrezia, who came to life five years later, were the most notable.

Pope Pius II died in 1464, and Rodrigo again influenced the decision of the election of the following pope: Pope Paul I. A few years later, Rodrigo was sent to Spain with the authority to either agree or disagree on the marriage of Ferdinand and Isabella. Approving their marriage would signal that he agrees with the union that would form between the Spanish regions Aragon and Castille; if he denies their marriage, he will deny the union between the regions.

Rodrigo accepted the marriage, earning King Ferdinand's support. He also used his position to name his son Duke and marry his daughters to build alliances. Instead of electing Rodrigo as pope, cardinals elected Innocent VIII. Rodrigo did everything he could to get to the throne. He even earned the support of Innocent, who resulted in a lot of chaos before he died. Rodrigo continued bribing people in positions of power until he finally bought himself the papacy. He was then renamed Pope Alexander VI.

Pope Alexander VI

Surprisingly, Pope Alexander VI gained the support of the public. Although he was a skilled diplomat, he led an ostentatious, hedonistic lifestyle. Alexander couldn't separate his position and wealth from his family, so his son was soon named cardinal. The rest of his family arrived and settled all over Italy to reap their share of the rewards. Although nepotism was common in the papacy, Alexander went very far in abusing his position.

He had various mistresses and affairs, which tainted the church's image. Further disorder ensued when his children started getting in trouble with the families they married into. Alexander tried to salvage the situation through negations, which involved marrying off Lucrezia, who was 12 at the time, to Giovanni Sforza. He later divorced the couple when Giovanni opposed him.

Alexander retired to a palace instead of choosing to flee when King Charles VIII of France invaded Italy. He believed he could negotiate a compromise that guaranteed his life along with an independent papacy. France seized control of Naples, and Alexander played a role in getting the rest of Italy to unite. However, he knew it was time to flee when King Charles returned to Rome.

Cesare Borgia

In 1498, Pope Alexander formed an alliance with the new French King, Louis XIII, granting Cesare the title Duke of Valence. Cesare also married into the King's family and earned an army. The Duke went back to Italy, embarking on a remarkable career path in the military, and never saw his pregnant wife and his soon-to-be child again.

Cesare's military success brought him power over his father, and those who wanted to set appointments with the papacy found it more economical to speak to him rather than Alexander. Cesare earned the title of Captain-General of the army of the church. However, many people attributed the death of Lucrezia's husband, along

Cesare's military success brought him power over his father.[11]

with other unsolved murders, to him. Cesare's conquests left the family under control of a large amount of land. Lucrezia was also sent to marry Alfonso d'Este to secure Cesare's strategy.

The Fall of the Borgias

Cesare soon recognized that his alliance with France was no longer beneficial. After he planned everything needed to break away, his father died of malaria in 1503. Alexander was his benefactor; his lands weren't united yet, and he was also very ill. Cesare was forced to flee after his enemies came back from exile to fight. The new pope arrested Cesare. He also threw out most of the Borgias from their positions and controlled the others. After Cesare was released, he went to Naples, where Ferdinand of Aragon arrested him again. He managed to escape two years later but ended up murdered in 1507 when he was only 31 at the time.

Lucrezia Borgia

Lucrezia made amends with her husband and his family. She also reconciled with her state, where she became regent and took up positions in court. She patronized several artists, creating a court with substantial beauty and culture. She oversaw the state even through war. She was loved among the people and died in 1519 when she was 39.

29. The Sforza of Milan: Warriors and Patrons

The Sforza family was first known by the name Attendoli. This humble Italian family produced who would later be among the two most popular fortunes, giving rise to a dynasty whose rulership lasted for nearly a century. The Attendoli were a wealthy family of farmers who only assumed the name Sforza, which translates to force, when Muzio Attendolo, the dynasty's founder, came by. Muzio and his son Francesco were both mercenary army commanders. Francesco was named Duke of Milan when he married Duke Filippo Maria Visconti's daughter, Bianca, in 1450.

Francesco Sforza: The Patron of Art and Architecture

Francesco and Biancagave gave birth to Galeazzo Maria Sforza in 1444. Three years later, Duke Filippo Visconti died without a legitimate male heir. The Milanese thought it was an opportunity to establish the Ambrosian Republic, which later fell due to a financial crisis. They hired Francesco to maintain order in Milan. However, he decided to take advantage of the situation and form an allegiance with Venice. He borrowed money from the Medici family to establish strong troops and besieged Milan until the new government surrendered in 1450.

He hired Filatrete, who wrote a treatise representing himself as an architect, and Francesco, the patron, conversed about an ideal city called Sforzinda. Francesco ordered the continuity of projects that the Visconti had already started and commissioned the creation of new ones. He continued supporting the construction of the Milan Cathedral and the Certosa di Pavia. He also commissioned the Ospedale Maggiore and a church in the monastery of the Santa Maria delle Grazie.

Galeazzo Maria Sforza

Galeazzo Maria Sforza proved to be a capable ruler after his father died in 1466. Although he was considered ostentatious, authoritarian, and extravagant, Galeazzo Maria was great at his job. He was responsible for many projects that supported the field of agriculture, such as the construction of irrigation and transportation canals and the introduction of rice cultivation. He also played a role in boosting commerce and encouraging the manufacture of textiles like wool and silk. Galeazzo also contributed to the enrichment of Milan's culture by patronizing several poets, musicians, scholars, and artists. Some inadequacies in his political strategy led to Milan's isolation. He also ended up murdered by three conspirators on Christmas.

Ludovico Sforza

Ludovico Sforza, Galeazzo's brother, played a great role in the advancement of arts and politics during the Renaissance. He married Beatrice d'Este, who died while giving birth to their two sons in 1497. Ludovico tried to establish an allegiance with France to destabilize his enemies by encouraging King Charles VIII to invade the rest of Italy. However, diplomacy wasn't his strongest suit, and his pact resulted in the French occupation of Milan in 1499. He eventually died while he was imprisoned by the French in 1508.

Despite his political downfall, Ludovico was a significant patron of the arts. He commissioned several major artists like Bramante and Leonardo da Vinci, who worked on several prominent projects like The Last Supper. He also commissioned numerous architectural projects, including renovating several Milanese churches and constructing the Piazza Ducale in Vigevano.

The Medici, Borgia, and Sforza are among the most significant families of the Italian Renaissance. Their power and contributions left a lasting influence on the region. The Medicis were generous patrons of the arts and pioneers of transformative financial concepts who transformed Florence into a cultural center. Although the Borgias were controversial, they played a key role in supporting several artists and scholars, and the Sforzas shaped Milan's political, architectural, and artistic landscape.

Chapter 7: Exploration and Expansion Stories

Expansion and exploration made the world feel a lot smaller and more accessible. Formations of new countries like the United States are because the age of exploration allowed for new cultures to uniquely form in different parts of the world. Furthermore, expansion, along with the development of new technology, is what created the globalized world that people live in today. As much as the adventuring spirit of those who discovered new parts of the world can be admired, the atrocities that were committed in the name of empires and religion cannot be overlooked.

Therefore, it is essential to honestly explore how the European world interacted with the indigenous people they encountered and how the wealth of the Western world grew due to exploration. The complex relationship between discovery and ethnic and religious identities can be told through the stories of the explorers who stepped out of Europe into the unknown. Looking into the details of expansion stories in the imperialist age can reveal how the world was divided and how it influenced modern culture. Colonization and conquering are central parts of European history that perfectly contrast the highest and lowest points of the human drive to explore.

30. Columbus and the Discovery of the New World

It is somewhat of a misnomer to claim that Christopher Columbus discovered the Americas; however, that does not detract from the incredible feat of expansion journeying into these unknown territories. Columbus was the first European to set foot in America. The continent's discovery helped Spain exponentially grow its wealth in the era. Furthermore, it was the beginning of the American project, which the world has seen grow into the international superpower it is today.

Christopher Columbus discovered the Americas.[12]

The sail routes to Asia, where valuable resources like spices could be traded, were controlled by the Ottoman Empire at the time. The Columbus voyage aimed to find a route to Asia by sailing west from Europe. Columbus was an Italian native, but his journey was sponsored by Spanish Catholic Monarchs who were inspired because they had defeated the Moors in Grenada. The renewed national spirit gave the Spanish Empire adventurous aspirations. On August 3rd, 1492, Columbus left the coast of Spain on three ships: the Santa Maria, the Pinta, and the Nina.

By October 12th, Columbus first encountered land in the Bahamas, which he believed to be the Indies. He named the island San Salvador and claimed it for Spain. Columbus's voyage continued as he reached Cuba, thinking it was mainland China. He traveled to Haiti and the Dominican Republic, mistakenly assuming the islands were Japan. He named the islands Hispaniola, where Columbus established a small colony of 39 men. In March 1493, the explorer finally returned to Spain with captives from the newfound lands as well as gold and spices. Columbus received the highest praise upon his return.

Columbus journeyed back to the New World another three times in 1493, 1498, and 1502, before he died in 1506. The gold that Columbus acquired made him a wealthy man, and the blueprint that he had set out helped transform Spain into one of the wealthiest nations in the century that followed. It can be argued that Europe would not have been able to establish itself as a global force without Columbus' brave venture into the New World. Columbus was one of the key figures in the Age of Exploration and is seen as an inspiration to many for venturing bravely into the unknown. His influence in the region he discovered can still be felt today, with Islands like Haiti and much of South America still being largely Catholic.

Although many honor Columbus as a great explorer and pioneer of European excellence, his accomplishments are not without controversy. Many today highlight that his treatment of Natives was atrocious and unacceptable. Since the Native people of the islands did not practice Catholicism, Columbus saw them as pagans who were worthy of ill-treatment in the name of the Lord. He saw himself as their superior who needed to religiously educate them. October 9th is celebrated as Columbus Day, but due to the controversies attached to his expansion of the Spanish Empire, some choose to celebrate it as Indigenous Day instead so that the native people could be honored as well.

31. Vasco Da Gama: Finding the Sea Route to India

Vasco Da Gama was the first European to find an ocean route from Europe to India. Da Gama's journey followed Bartholomew Dias, who had sailed along the coast of West Africa to what is now known as South Africa from Portugal. Dias applied to complete the journey rounding the Southern tip of Africa to India, but the Crown put Da Gama in charge of the voyage. The journey's goal was to avoid the land-bound trade routes that had historically been used for commerce between Africa, the Middle East, and the Italians. Furthermore, the Da Gama and the Portuguese crown believed they could ally with Christian nations against the Middle East and North African Islamic empires.

Vasco Da Gama was the first European to find an ocean route from Europe to India.[13]

Da Gama's expedition commenced in 1497. He arrived on the Southwest coast of India in 1498. Two new ships were built for Da Gama's treacherous journey, with an additional two being added. Da Gama captained the Sao Gabriel, and his brother Paulo Coelho was in charge of the Sao Rapahel. The biggest of the four ships was captained by another one of Da Gama's brothers, Nicolau

Coelho. The third ship was called the Berrio and was able to carry 200 tons of merchandise. The large size of the Berrio can draw a picture of how large the operation was intended to be to exploit this newly carved-out trade route.

Dias's strategy differed from Da Gama's insofar as he stayed close to the coastline, battling the rough waters and raging winds, while Da Gama strayed off further into the ocean, where he made use of winds that favored their journey. When Da Gama reached Southern Africa on November 22nd in the area now known as Mossel Bay, the crew decided that they would dismantle the biggest ship and split the supplies and crew between the three ships that remained.

Sailing in those days was no easy feat. The crew subsisted on hardened biscuits that they would bang against the hard wooden floors of the ships to get the bugs out. These almost inedible biscuits were supplemented with a dash of olive oil and a splash of water. They would then have salted beef or pork on some days; on other days, it was rice or cheese on the menu. Only the highest-ranking members of the crew were allowed to enjoy some dried fruit. The nutrient-scarce diet resulted in many crew members developing scurvy, a disease caused by a lack of vitamin C. When they reached the East Coast of Africa in Mobassa on April 7th, they were assisted by locals who knew how to cure the disease. The crew members suffering from scurvy were given oranges before fully recovering to continue the mission.

Da Gama arrived in India on May 18th, 1498. Their ships were fully loaded with rare spices like pepper and cinnamon before they made their journey back to Europe. Many more crew members died from scurvy on the way back because they were unable to get treated this time around. The second voyage Da Gam made in 1502 was less diplomatic as the explorer came with blood on his mind. The region was conquered, and Da Gama was crowned as the Viceroy of Portugal in the area. The work of Vaco Da Gama and Christopher Columbus propelled Europe into the age of imperialism, as many nations from the continent began conquering the world.

32. The Treaty of Tordesillas: Dividing the World

The Treaty of Tordesillas was signed to divide the Americas between two of the biggest superpowers at the time, Spain and Portugal. The discoveries of Columbus meant that there were new opportunities for empires to expand to grow their influence and wealth. Since these new territories were unclaimed in the European world, it opened the door for conflicts and disagreements. The Catholic Church had a lot of power at the time, so the Spanish rulers Queen Isabella I and King Ferdinand II sought help from Pope Alexander VI to make claims on these new lands without interference from Portugal or any other powerful Christian kingdoms.

The Pope issued a Papal bull that drew a dividing line that spanned about 320 miles west of the Cape Verde Islands. Spain was permitted to claim any lands west of the line, while Portugal was able to conquer lands east of the demarcation. Furthermore, the Pope declared that any lands owned by the Church were not to be touched. King John II was dissatisfied with the agreement because he believed that the bull tied his kingdom's hands in terms of claiming newly discovered land in the new world that Columbus had revealed. Moreover, the King claimed that there was not enough space at sea to freely move between the African continent and Europe.

To address the concerns of the Portuguese Empire, a meeting was set up in Tordesillas, Spain. Ambassadors from Spain and Portugal agreed to shift the dividing line to 1185 miles west of Cape Verde. In 1506, Pope Julius II sanctioned the change of the positioning of the line. This shift allowed Portugal to conquer Brazil, which was later discovered by Pedro Alvarez Cabral (This is why modern Brazilians are Portuguese speakers; the Portuguese territory was expanded inland into South America.)

Since the native populations of the Americas were not Christian, they were allowed to be conquered. The stipulation that Pope Alexander VI added meant that Spain and Portugal were not allowed to overthrow any Christian kings. The treaty was between Spain and Portugal, so the agreement did not consider other European empires like the British and Dutch. However, other European superpowers only claimed lands in the new world much later on. Considering that indigenous cultures like the Aztecs, Inca, and Tainos did not have a Christian king, they violently suffered during this colonial period.

33. Conquistadors and the Fall of Empires: The Aztecs and Incas

The Incan Empire was formed by conquering neighboring tribes in Peru. In 1533, the empire spanned vast lands and was the largest in the world. Like their European counterparts, the Inca used religion to conquer because their cosmology asserted that they had a divine right to rule. The Inca believed they were chosen people descended from their Sun deity, Inti. The Incas were on the brink of collapse when the explorer and conquistador Francisco Pizarro entered the picture. The conquered tribes under the Incan Empire could not integrate, which caused civil unrest, and European diseases that the Incas had no immunity to were ravaging the population.

Pizarro and his Spanish forces were able to defeat the Inca easily due to the superior European weapons, as well as the local inclination to rebel against their Incan oppressors. The collaboration with local warriors resulted in the Europeans being able to overthrow the powerful Incan Empire in one generation. The Inca had vast riches and dwelled in resource-filled Peru. Therefore, the conquistadors had ample motivation to conquer the region.

Francisco Pizarro and his partner Diego de Almagro had not achieved the renown that they yearned for in their own country as adventurers and treasure hunters. The discovery of South American riches was an opportunity for the two to make a name for themselves. They had seen how other conquistadors made fortunes in Mexico, so they aimed to emulate and recreate that success. The political instability among the Inca resulted in Spain being able to conquer the area by 1514; however, the transition was not smooth because the Spanish also experienced internal fighting that caused the murder of Pizarro.

Similar to the Inca, the Aztecs were also a conquering nation. The nation controlled about 500 different states who were required to pay tributes to their Aztec rulers. Furthermore, the Aztecs practiced human sacrifice, which bred resentment among some of the groups under the empire. Hernan Cortes was able to practice diplomacy to get the support of rebel forces under various chiefs. They captured the Aztec capital of Tenochtitlan with the help of local fighters. Smallpox also played a big role in devastating much of the indigenous population.

The historical drama did not end when Cortes took over the capital. A group of Spaniards were sent over to Mexico with orders to arrest Cortes when they arrived. Cortes defeated the arresting party with a surprise attack and convinced many of the soldiers to help him with his ambitions to conquer the Aztec Empire. However, Officer Pedro de Alvarado, whom Cortes had left in charge, had massacred many of the Aztec people while the leaders were gone. De Alvarado's actions caused the locals to rebel. Emperor Montezuma, who was Cortes's Aztec ally, was commanded to put an end to the rebellion immediately, but he had lost favor with his people and was unable to influence them effectively. The Emperor died trying to stop the unrest. Eventually, the Aztec Empire completely collapsed under Spanish rule because of the superior European weaponry and the death caused by foreign diseases. This is why modern Mexicans speak Spanish.

34. The Slave Trade: A Dark Chapter in Exploration

The transatlantic slave trade is one of the darkest stains on the development of the Western world. The dehumanizing atrocities committed during the slave trade are almost unimaginable in the modern world, where people are protected by human rights considerations. Slavery was a common practice when the transatlantic slave trade began bringing people of African descent to the Caribbean, as well as the Americas. The trade of humans spanned from the sixteenth to the nineteenth century. Much of the economies of European nations were propped up with the trade of enslaved people, so African people were an integral part of the European story at its foundation.

Many people have an unrealistic image of how the slave trade took place. Europeans did not run into Africa, rounding up people to sell. Slave traders bartered with Africans who captured enslaved people and would trade with them for metals, ammunition, beads, and other goods. In 1444, Portuguese marauders aimed to go into Senegal with their superior weapons to capture enslaved people in the country. However, the Senegalese people were avid sailors and were able to outmaneuver the Europeans in the shallow waters off the coast. Therefore, the Portuguese slave traders were forced to trade with the African locals as opposed to using military action. As the European demand for enslaved people increased, they began fuelling wars between rival groups in Africa, facilitating the capturing of more people to sell. It is estimated that the entire slave trade captured over 15 million Africans. Furthermore, multiple generations were born into captivity and traded as commodities.

The slave trade was justified by religion, as many pastors preached sermons about how men have dominion over beasts. In this perception of the world, enslaved Africans were seen as animals that could be likened to livestock. This dehumanization of enslaved Africans resulted in terrible treatment as they were beaten, tortured, and sometimes fought for the entertainment of their European masters. The negative impacts of the slave trade are still being experienced today, as many people in the African diaspora have lower socioeconomic positions in society globally. This social impact is a result of generational oppression derailing the development of African people abroad while colonization destabilized people on the continent.

Exploration, expansion, and colonization are complex topics to fully unpack. Much of what is enjoyed in the developed world is a result of this conquest. Without this chapter in history, Europe and the United States as we know it today may have never existed. However, some of the problems that the developing world is still dealing with today are a direct result of slavery and colonization. Therefore, a knife's edge has to be walked between the adventuring heroes that are honored and celebrated and the condemnation of some of their darker actions.

A mistake many people make is weighing past actions against the moral or ethical standards that we have now. The age of conquest was a different period when people had a completely foreign way of understanding the world compared to modern sensibilities. Therefore, as much as condemnation is due for the murderous, genocidal, and oppressive actions of European travelers, conquerors, and settlers, it is also important to note that it was a step toward developing the more humane perceptions people have now.

The bravery it took to venture out into an unknown world on treacherous seas, experiencing untold discomfort, is admirable. The people who had the guts to go out on these journeys of discovery must not be forgotten, but in the same breath, the cultures that suffered under European oppression must also be uplifted as central to the European story. The tales of Europe expanding into the globe are a balance of the adventuring spirit building new ways of life worldwide while oppressing people who were different from them.

Chapter 8: Enlightenment, Retribution, and Revolution Stories

From the late 17th to the early 19th century, a series of uprisings and revolutions marked Europe's history. This chapter aims to capture the transformative period known as the Enlightenment and how its ideas fueled social and political revolts. Also known as the "Age of Reason," the period of Enlightenment brought on new philosophies that challenged traditional authority and embraced reason, liberty, and progress, shaping philosophical, political, and scientific discourse.

Renowned thinkers of this era created a massive change in reforming thinking and reason, laying the foundation for modern thought. Imagine centuries of traditional beliefs being set aside in just a few decades. This is what the Enlightenment was like. Instead of age-old customs, it gave way to individualism, exploration, scientific discoveries, tolerance, and political and industrial revolutions.

Thinkers of the Enlightenment were inspired by ancient Roman and Greek civilizations.[14]

The origins of this period can be traced back to the aftermath of the English Civil Wars. During this time, the power of the ever-present autocratic monarchy was restored, beginning with giving back the reign to Charles II in 1660. This fueled dissatisfaction among the political thinkers at the time, who now began to consider the many ways the country would benefit from different political and societal structures. Their ideas launched movements demanding political change, which eventually occurred in 1688/89 when William and Mary were given the throne (known as the Glorious Revolution).

Thinkers of the Enlightenment were inspired by ancient Roman and Greek civilizations, citing how modern society would benefit from modeling these. It was an undeniably different idea from the centuries of political tyranny and dissolution of personal rights and well-being people experienced across Europe. John Locke, an English physician and philosopher, saw the answer in the separation of the government and the church. He believed this would encourage religious toleration, fighting for people's rights and property ownership (proposing an early form of social contract between people and the state).

Locke also claimed that human consciousness was the gateway to true liberty, and he dismissed the ancient (but highly prevailing at the time) notion that knowledge is an elusive and secretive entity and could only be obtained through mystical ways. Locke's ideas reflected the beliefs of Thomas Hobbes, who also advocated for social contracts between the people and the government, seeing it as the key to people's contentment. Grand promises notwithstanding, these ideas and the revolution they caused often faced retribution from the old regimes.

35. Voltaire: Champion of Enlightenment and Free Thought

Voltaire (born François-Marie Arouet) was a pivotal figure in the Enlightenment. He was a prolific French writer, philosopher, and historian. Through his versatile career, he advocated for freedom of speech and faith. He also supported the notion of creating a divide between the government and the church. In the age of aristocratic tyranny, this wasn't a small feat. Voltaire had to fight against the French censorship laws that prohibited the publication of anything that went against the ideas of the Church or the main French political institutions.

Fortunately, Voltaire was very clever, as illustrated by the following story. Once, he returned an insult to a nobleman and was arrested despite not being the one initiating the conflict. He managed to negotiate his release from the Bastille and got himself exiled to England instead. Witnessing the benefits of Britain's constitutional monarchy, Voltaire became even more passionate about freedom of speech and personal liberty.

From England, Voltaire continued to critique the French state and the Church's power over it. He wrote several novels ridiculing the government, religion, theologians, and everything and everyone oppressing the commoners. In them, Voltaire argued the unfairness of the fact that the latter had to shoulder the burden of taxation while nobility, officials, and church officials were exempt. One of his recurring themes was a hero going through unimaginable hurdles only to have them reassured by noblemen that it was for their benefit.

Some credit his prolific creativity to his excessive caffeine consumption (he reportedly could drink up to 70 cups of coffee a day!) Whatever was behind his thoughts and beliefs, Voltaire became a true champion of freedom in Britain and America. His principles become widely recognized and accepted across other developed countries as well. However, not all countries were on board with allowing freedom of religious expression. Some would imprison and execute those who publicly spoke about these new, revolutionary, enlightened ideas – as well as those accused of doing so. Voltaire knew that in some countries, states, and religions, united would always oppress the freedom of independent thinking. However, until his death, he continued to encourage people to oppose these violent and oppressive regimes, not allowing them to silence anyone who disagreed with their way of thinking.

36. The Social Contract: Rousseau's Revolutionary Idea

After Locke and others popularized the idea of social contracts, the concurrent requests for political change in France at the dawn of the 18th century pushed the notion forward. Diderot, for example, claimed that by expanding reason (provided by a contract in which the state allows people to develop independent and critical thinking), people would be able to keep destructive passions in check and maintain their virtue.

A similar idea was proclaimed by Jean-Jacques Rousseau, who argued that people were rational by birth. However, when they lost their freedom due to societal constraints, their reason was suppressed, and they became unable to think rationally. Moreover, civilized society made people unhappy, and to change this, people should seek closeness with nature, away from the oppressive society.

Rousseau also claimed that true political sovereignty was possible – but could only be obtained by people when the laws were adequately maintained and the rulings respected. This thought was expressed in one of Rousseu's most renowned works, The Social Contract, in which he argued that people could only be free if their society granted them certain rights and ensured their well-being. This required a democratic government, which was a radical political notion at the time. However, in just a few decades, the same idea influenced some of the most significant revolutionary movements, including the famous French Revolution. Even revolutionaries like Robespierre were inspired by Rousseu's works and philosophy.

For the same reason, they were blamed by the French government for terrible acts they never committed. Despite this, The Social Contract became one of European political history's most influential pieces of literature. To this day, the ideas it dissects continue to inspire by emphasizing the importance of being a responsible part of society to ensure liberty and well-being.

37. The Storming of the Bastille: Spark of the French Revolution

By the summer of 1789, France was well on its way to a full-blown revolution. The governor of the Bastille – the fortress that served as the most infamous prison at the time – knew that the revolutionaries could target the building and asked for help. He had reasons to fear defeat. The guardians of the fortress were mere veterans no longer capable of serving in the battle. A few more capable soldiers arrived, but there were also uncontrollable protests in the city several days beforehand. After that, the Bastille received reinforcements of 250 barrels of gunpowder, distributed among the guards as they raised the drawbridges. Unfortunately, this was proven to be a little too late. When they heard that King Luis was planning to arrest the brand new National Assembly that promised more power to people, the Parisians got infuriated. On July 14, 1789, they armed themselves with swords, muskets, and other makeshift weapons and began to gather around the fortress.

Reports account for nine hundred Parisians gathering outside the fortress that morning, led by three delegates from the Hôtel de Ville (the seat of city government), who presented the rebel's demands. Not wanting to do the dishonorable act of capitulating before the enemy without authorization from the King, the governor refused to surrender at first. However, he withdrew the cannons from the walls to show he had no intention of inflicting harm on anyone. One of the delegates saw this with their own eyes and went to announce it to the mob, but it was too late. By the time they returned down to the base of the fortress, two agile revolutionaries had climbed the walls and cut the chain of the drawbridge, causing it to fall. From then on, there was no way to de-escalate the situation. People would become trapped and die under the bridge, while others started to run across into the yard. They were under the misconception that the guards let them in. However, the guards knew nothing about this, and when they saw the crowd surging in, they began to shoot in panic. In turn, the people thought that they'd been lured into a trap, and those with weapons proceeded to attack.

While the revolutionaries were fighting the guards of the Bastille, the French Guards' rebellious members and other defecting soldiers heard of what was happening and joined the battle. Their organization was a little haphazard, but they brought valuable reinforcement to the crowd, including cannons they fired at the Bastille's gate. While the governor still considered a counterattack at this time, his men talked him out of it. Seeing no other option but to surrender, the governor raised the white flag and let the other drawbridge down. After all, he had no backup. The royal army fled the city by this time, trying to get as far ahead as possible to avoid the mob reaching them, eventually settling in Versailles, where the King resided.

After flooding the Bastille, the revolutionaries liberated the prisoners, disarmed the remaining guards (several of them died or were lynched during or immediately after the attack), and seized the ammunition. The governor's leading officers were killed, and he was taken to the Hôtel de Ville, where his future punishment was to be determined. However, not wanting anyone else to decide his fate, the governor provoked one of his captors to attack and kill him.

When the news of the Bastille's siege reached King Louis XVI in Versailles, he made a last attempt to stop the revolution. He returned to function the Jacques Necker, the chief minister whom he removed for not preventing the rise of the National Assembly. However, the reversal of this decision didn't satisfy the crowd anymore. With the fall of the Bastille, the revolution officially started, and there was no stopping it now. Four years later, shortly after the French monarchy was abolished, King Louis and his wife Marie Antoinette were captured and executed for treason.

As the revolution began, there were talks about turning the Bastille into a museum or even a base for volunteers. However, with the building's past and sheer size, the Permanent Committee of Municipal Electors couldn't justify its upkeep anymore (it was hardly worth it before, given the small number of prisoners it housed) and authorized its demolition. A park was built in its place, standing as a homage to Parisians' first victory during the revolution. However, the people weren't left without tangible memories of this event (despite sacking the idea of the museum). Wanting to promote the victory and its significance, one of the people doing the demolition seized some of the Bastille remains and converted them into souvenirs. The different items seized were sold quickly. Fans from its papers were the ladies' favorites, while gentlemen preferred paperweights from the rocks once held up the fortress. There were even miniature replicas of the building to buy. People from other parts of France came to Paris to get a good deal on the Bastille stones. They took these home, inspired to contribute to the revolution themselves.

Today, the fortress's outline and a small portion of the foundation remain a symbol of how people joining forces brought an end to a failing regime and gave momentum to the French revolutionary rationale.

38. The Declaration of Rights of Man and Citizen: A Revolutionary Document

No narrative of the Enlightenment would be complete without mentioning the Declaration of the Rights of Man and the Citizen. Issued on 26th August 1789 by the French National Constituent Assembly, under the original name of *Déclaration des droits de l'homme et du citoyen*, this was the first document clearly outlining the individual and collective rights of people during the French Revolution. The document's creators took inspiration from constitutional pieces like the Magna Carta and the revolutionary ideas spreading across the United States, which led to the signing of the Declaration of Independence. There were unmistakable differences. For example, The Declaration of the Rights of Man and the Citizen emphasizes that people's rights are universal and inviolable and should come naturally to be upheld.

However, the influence of the Magna Carta was undeniable. Declaration of the Rights of Man and the Citizen also talks about making monarch subordinates to the law, proclaims that no one should be arrested, imprisoned, or accused without lawfully established causes, and mandates that taxation will require common consent. The authors also worked with Thomas Jefferson in the past, who inspired the Magna Carta and left his mark on the Declaration of the Rights of Man and the Citizen. This was seen in the clause talking about the innate freedom of people and the need for them to remain this way, thus having equal rights.

39. Immanuel Kant: Reason and Enlightenment

Influenced by Rousseau and Descartes, German philosopher Immanuel Kant was another remarkable character during the Enlightenment. Born and raised in Koenigsberg (modern-day Russia) in 1781, Kant began publishing works that laid the foundations for modern philosophy. As his publications began to mount, he likened his efforts to enlighten people to that of Copernicus, and rightfully so. He inspired many other philosophers – whose work was simply called post-Kantian.

However, Kant's road to success in modernizing philosophy wasn't exactly smooth. When he began to explore the scene, there were two major camps of European thinkers. The empiricists, like Hume, Locke, Bacon, and Berkeley, prevailed in Britain. Whereas the rationalists ruled the rest of the continent. Their

IMMANUEL KANT
From a painting

Kant was influenced by Rousseau and Descartes.[15]

ranks included Spinoza, Leibniz, and Descartes. They claimed that a belief must be certified through reasoning to be seen as knowledge. This included inferential steps from unshakable principles —either self-evident to whoever observed them or couldn't be denied. According to the rationalist, these axioms already exist in everyone. In other words, every person was born with the innate ability to recognize them. By contrast, empiricists considered this idea an illusion. They argued that knowledge can only be obtained through hard work and experience – when people use their senses to consolidate new information into their minds. However, this information is bound to be inaccurate and subject to change due to future learning experiences.

In a never-before-seen move, Kant found a way to consolidate rationalist and empirical ideas into one solid thought form. Many describe his way of incorporating their strongest aspects while displaying their inadequacies radically revamping. At first, he was heavily criticized for turning the centuries-old traditional beliefs on their head. However, as other great thinkers dived deeper into his reasoning, more and more people ruled out the conventional concerns. Soon, they didn't even find them worth pursuing during philosophical debates discussing the nature of knowledge.

The reasoning behind Kant's reformative ideas and methods was also shocking at the time – given it was connected to metaphysical principles (Kant bound philosophy to science). The followers of the ancient traditions his ideas pushed aside and modernist thinkers at the time both disregarded the notion that people's knowledge could be tied to external objects. While some played with the concept of "objects of knowledge," most found their existence unimaginable. It was common sense to think that the subject of knowledge would exist separately from physical objects – except Kant disagreed. Inspired by Copernicus's idea that the earth circles around the sun and not the other way around (as it was believed at the time), Kant proposed to change the assumption that people's knowledge can transcend the nature of objects and consider that the objects can conform to peoples way of acquiring knowledge. This required inverted thinking – just as astronomers had to invert their theory of the sun and earth to resolve the difficulties they encountered during their research. In other words, by changing perspectives, the notion of the objects of knowledge wouldn't seem unimaginable anymore.

The above recounting of Kant's work is only a snippet of its effort toward expanding the philosophies revolving around reason. Another example can be found in his publication titled "What is Enlightenment?" in which he attempted to answer age-old questions troubling thinkers. They lived in it for a while now, yet they couldn't define it. According to Kant, the Enlightenment is nothing but one's way of breaking free of a state of unknowing and being led by others and their knowledge. It's like a child starting to use his reason and understanding to learn what he needs to survive and thrive as he grows into adulthood. It's not letting someone else tell you how and what to think. It's having the courage to break free from others' tutelage and use the reason you were born with. Don't think you can't do it and make up your mind. Don't be afraid to come to your own resolutions.

Kant argued that following one's own reason leads to a faculty shared by all able-minded people on earth. If one also accepts his notion that reason is an innate capacity rather than a learned skill, the conclusion is simple. Everyone can learn the same things in the same way.

By putting this idea in the essay *"What Is Enlightenment?"* in front of the general public, Kant took a massive risk. He had his reputation as a renowned philosopher at stake, and this wasn't a notion everyone was prepared to embrace. Fortunately, with this work – along with his other publication, *"Critique of Pure* Reason"- he was able to not only uphold but further grow the number of his supporters across Europe. While these works were published in Berlin, his assumptions were shared by many and were seen on the other side of the continent as well – including some of the central characters of the French Revolution that was soon to follow.

Chapter 9: Napoleon Bonaparte: Stories of His Rise and Fall

Napoleon Bonaparte, the diminutive dynamo of the 19th century, was a man whose stature may have been short but whose ambitions reached towering heights. With a penchant for conquering both territory and hearts, this Corsican-born general-turned-emperor reshaped the map of Europe and redefined the art of warfare. You can't learn about Europe's history without coming across this influential figure. His cunning strategies were as sharp as his iconic bicorne hat, and his charisma, like a fine French wine, left a lasting impression on history. Whether you view him as a military genius or a power-hungry conqueror, one thing is certain: Napoleon was a figure who refused to be confined by the limits of his stature, leaving an indelible mark on the world stage. You can admire his audacity or question his audaciousness, but there's no denying that Napoleon Bonaparte was a man who knew how to make history dance to his imperial tune.

Napoleon refused to be confined by the limits of his stature.[16]

40. Napoleon: From Corsica to Emperor

In his early years, Napoleon Bonaparte, known as Napoleone di Buonaparte, came into the world on August 15th, 1769, in the picturesque town of Ajaccio on the island of Corsica. Napoleon's family occupied a unique social niche between the haute bourgeoisie and minor nobility. His ancestry was a subject of speculation, with Napoleon dismissing extravagant claims and asserting his Corsican roots. Napoleon's Corsican heritage with Italian roots became a target for detractors who sought to tarnish his image. Early British biographer William Burdon attributed his character's supposed "dark ferocity" to his Italian ancestry, unfairly likening him to Italian treachery rather than embracing French openness and vivacity. The British journalist William Cobbett even dismissed him as a "low-bred upstart from the contemptible island of Corsica." Yet, despite these prejudices, Napoleon's actions defied stereotypes.

At nine, Napoleon's father secured their family's recognition as Corsican nobility, enabling him to apply for royal bursaries for his sons' education. Napoleon's journey to becoming a French officer and gentleman was set in motion when he received one of these bursaries, allowing him to embark on his education in France. Napoleon excelled in mathematics, a subject he later found crucial for military leadership. Napoleon's exceptional intellect and aptitude for mathematics led him to choose a career in the prestigious artillery rather than the navy. He excelled academically, impressing his teachers and receiving recommendations for further education in prestigious institutions. His decision to join the artillery marked him as part of an elite group, and he became the first Corsican to attend the École Royale Militaire in Paris.

Napoleon completed his studies at Brienne and entered the École Royale Militaire in Paris in 1784. On September 1st, 1785, Napoleon received his commission into the Compagnie d'Autume of bombardiers within the 5th Brigade of the 1st Battalion of the Régiment de la Fère, stationed at Valence on the left bank of the Rhône. At just sixteen, he was among the youngest officers and the only Corsican holding an artillery commission in the French army. By late May 1788, Napoleon was stationed at the School of Artillery in Auxonne, eastern France, not far from Dijon.

In April 1789, he was sent to Seurre to help put down a riot, showing his willingness to maintain order and discipline. This is when his career truly began. However, the political situation in France was rapidly evolving, leading to the outbreak of the French Revolution on July 14, 1789, with the storming of the Bastille. Napoleon's reign was defined by his military conquests. One of Napoleon's most celebrated achievements was his series of Italian campaigns in the late 1790s. His military brilliance was on full display as he defeated a series of Austrian and Italian armies, expanding French territory and establishing new republics in the process. These campaigns showcased his tactical genius and his ability to inspire his troops. The famous "Whiff of Grapeshot" in 1795, where he quelled a Parisian mob, further solidified his reputation as a military savior.

In 1799, the political landscape of France shifted dramatically. The Directory, the existing government, was beset by corruption and instability. In a coup d'état known as the 18 Brumaire, Napoleon overthrew the Directory and established the Consulate, with himself as First Consul. This marked the beginning of his effective rule over France. In 1804, he declared himself Emperor of the French, effectively ending the French Revolution's egalitarian ideals. His coronation at Notre Dame Cathedral in Paris was a grand spectacle, showcasing his power and influence. As Emperor, he implemented numerous reforms that modernized France, including the Napoleonic Code, which laid the foundation for many modern legal systems.

41. The Napoleonic Code: A Legal Legacy

Napoleon's ascent to power in France in the late 18th century coincided with the tumultuous era of the French Revolution. With the old legal system in disarray, legal reform was urgently needed. Napoleon recognized this opportunity to consolidate his power and establish a legal code that would underpin his rule. He appointed a commission of jurists, headed by Jean-Jacques Régis de Cambacérès, to draft a comprehensive civil code.

The Napoleonic Code introduced several groundbreaking principles that continue to shape modern legal systems:

- **Clarity and Simplicity:** The code aimed to provide a clear and concise set of laws, doing away with the complexity and ambiguity characteristic of the feudal legal systems of the time. It prioritized simplicity and accessibility, making the law comprehensible to the common citizen.

- **Equality before the Law:** This code emphasized the principle of equality, stating that all citizens were equal before the law. This was a significant departure from the privileges and inequalities that had characterized the Ancien Régime.

- **Property Rights**: It protected private property rights, reinforcing the idea that individuals had a right to possess, use, and dispose of their property as they saw fit. This provision was influential in the development of capitalist economies.

- **Freedom of Contract:** The Napoleonic Code supported freedom of contract, allowing individuals to enter into agreements based on their own volition. This laid the foundation for modern contract law.

- **Family Law**: The code reformed family law by allowing divorce, granting fathers greater authority over their children, and simplifying inheritance rules.

In addition to the Napoleonic Code, Napoleon's rule in France was marked by wide-ranging reforms that transformed the country in various ways:

- **Educational Reforms:** Napoleon recognized the importance of education in building a strong nation. He established a public education system known as the Napoleonic University, which provided education from elementary to university levels. This system aimed to produce skilled bureaucrats and professionals.

- **Administrative Reforms:** To streamline governance, Napoleon centralized administrative power. He divided France into departments, each with a prefect appointed by the central government. This structure improved efficiency and control.

- **Legal Reforms:** Beyond the Napoleonic Code, legal reforms included the establishment of the Council of State, which acted as a legal advisory body and helped standardize laws and regulations.
- **Financial Reforms**: Napoleon stabilized France's finances by introducing the franc as the national currency and establishing the Bank of France. These measures contributed to economic stability.
- **Religious Reforms:** Napoleon signed the Concordat with the Catholic Church in 1801, reconciling state and church relations. While Catholicism was recognized as the dominant religion, religious freedom was guaranteed.

The Napoleonic Code and the wide-ranging reforms instituted by Napoleon in France represent a significant turning point in legal, social, and administrative history. These reforms modernized France and had a lasting influence on other countries and legal systems worldwide. The principles of equality, clarity, and rationality in the Napoleonic Code continue to shape modern legal systems, emphasizing the enduring legacy of Napoleon's era of reform.

42. Austerlitz: Napoleon's Greatest Victory

On December 2nd, 1805, the Battle of Austerlitz, fought between the French army led by Emperor Napoleon Bonaparte and the combined forces of the Russian Empire and the Holy Roman Empire, unfolded on the icy plains near the town of Austerlitz in what is now the Czech Republic. This battle is often regarded as Napoleon's greatest military triumph, showcasing his tactical brilliance and earning him the title of a military genius.

To appreciate the significance of Austerlitz, it's essential to understand the strategic backdrop of the Napoleonic Wars. In 1805, the Third Coalition, comprising Russia, Austria, and the United Kingdom, had formed with the aim of defeating Napoleon's French Empire, which had been expanding rapidly across Europe. The Allies planned to encircle and crush Napoleon's Grande Armée, setting the stage for the Battle of Austerlitz.

Napoleon recognized the danger posed by the superior numbers of the Allied armies. He initiated a strategic retreat to lure them into a vulnerable position, drawing the Allies deeper into France. This maneuver gave him time to consolidate his forces and choose the battlefield. Napoleon selected the Pratzen Heights near Austerlitz as the battleground. He realized that these heights held the key to victory. He deliberately weakened his right flank to draw the Allies into a decisive confrontation, making it appear vulnerable. A thick fog covered the battlefield on the morning of the battle, obscuring visibility. Napoleon recognized this as an advantage and waited until the fog lifted, preventing the Allies from fully assessing his forces' disposition.

Believing Napoleon's right flank was weak, the Allies launched a massive assault on that sector. However, this played into Napoleon's hands, as he had concentrated his forces in the center and left. Napoleon ordered a devastating counterattack as the Allies committed their forces to the attack. The French infantry, under Marshal Soult, assaulted the weakened Allied center, splitting their forces in two. Meanwhile, Marshal Davout held the Pratzen Heights with a smaller force. His tenacity and the foggy conditions delayed the Allies' realization that the heights had not been abandoned. Once the fog cleared, it was too late, and Napoleon's forces held the crucial high ground.

The Battle of Austerlitz ended in a resounding victory for Napoleon. The Allies suffered heavy casualties and were forced to retreat. This triumph not only solidified Napoleon's reputation as a military genius but also led to the signing of the Treaty of Pressburg, which greatly favored France and dismantled the Holy Roman Empire. Austerlitz marked the pinnacle of Napoleon's military career.

43. Napoleon's Russian Catastrophe: The Retreat from Moscow

The retreat from Moscow in 1812 stands as one of the most catastrophic and infamous episodes in military history. Emperor Napoleon Bonaparte, who had once been the master of Europe, led his Grande Armée into Russia with grand ambitions of conquest. However, as the Russian campaign unfolded, it became clear that it would be a brutal and ultimately disastrous endeavor.

By 1812, Napoleon's French Empire was at its zenith. With most of Europe under his control, he sought to expand his influence in Russia. His ambition was to compel the Russian Tsar, Alexander I, to adhere to the Continental System, an economic blockade against British trade. For this, Napoleon assembled a colossal army, often referred to as the Grande Armée, consisting of over 600,000 soldiers from various European nations under his control. In June 1812, they crossed the Neman River and entered Russian territory.

The Russian army, under Field Marshal Mikhail Kutuzov, opted to engage Napoleon at the Battle of Borodino in September 1812. This brutal conflict was one of the bloodiest of the Napoleonic Wars, with heavy casualties. While the French emerged victorious, their losses were staggering. After the costly battle, Napoleon's forces entered Moscow in September 1812. However, the Russian army had employed a scorched-earth strategy, leaving the city abandoned and in flames. Napoleon had no choice but to occupy a ruined, depopulated Moscow. As winter descended upon Russia, the situation for the French grew dire. The harsh Russian winter, coupled with dwindling supplies and the vast distances they had to traverse, took a heavy toll on Napoleon's army.

Realizing that remaining in Moscow was unsustainable, Napoleon ordered the retreat in late October 1812. This retreat would prove to be a nightmarish ordeal. The Grande Armée faced extreme hardships during the retreat. Starvation, frostbite, and constant harassment by Russian forces further depleted their numbers. Thousands perished from exhaustion and hunger. One of the most desperate moments came at the Bérézina River in November 1812. The French had to cross the freezing river while under relentless Russian attacks. Many drowned or were killed during this crossing.

By the time Napoleon and his shattered army crossed back into friendly territory, only a fraction of the once-mighty Grande Armée remained. Estimates of casualties vary, but it is believed that only around 10% of the invading force survived. The retreat from Moscow marked a turning point in Napoleon's fortunes. The catastrophic losses severely weakened his grip on Europe, and it marked the beginning of his eventual downfall. The disaster in Russia galvanized the other European powers against Napoleon. A Sixth Coalition was formed, and a series of campaigns known as the War of the Sixth Coalition would ultimately lead to Napoleon's defeat and exile.

44. Waterloo: The End of an Era

The Battle of Waterloo, fought on June 18th, 1815, near the town of Waterloo in present-day Belgium, stands as a pivotal moment in history. It marked the culmination of a series of conflicts known as the Napoleonic Wars and, more significantly, the end of an era dominated by one of history's most iconic figures, Emperor Napoleon Bonaparte. This epic battle pitted the French forces under Napoleon against the combined armies of the Seventh Coalition, led by the Duke of Wellington and Prussian Field Marshal Gebhard Leberecht von Blücher.

Napoleon's defeat in Russia encouraged the formation of the Sixth Coalition, comprising Britain, Russia, Prussia, and Austria. The Coalition launched a successful campaign in 1814 that culminated in the capture of Paris. Facing pressure from his marshals and a lack of support, Napoleon abdicated on April 6th, 1814. He was exiled to the island of Elba, and Louis XVIII was restored to the French throne. Napoleon's exile was short-lived. On February 26th, 1815, he escaped from Elba and returned to France. This event marked the beginning of the Hundred Days when he reclaimed power and declared himself Emperor again.

Napoleon moved swiftly to raise a new army and launch a pre-emptive strike against the coalition forces assembling in Belgium. His strategy was to divide and defeat the allied armies before they could unite. On June 16th, 1815, Napoleon engaged the Prussian army under Blücher at the Battle of Ligny. The French emerged victorious, but the Prussians managed an organized retreat, setting the stage for critical development. Simultaneously, a minor engagement occurred at Quatre Bras, where the French sought to prevent the British under Wellington from linking up with the Prussians. It ended inconclusively.

On June 18th, 1815, the main confrontation occurred at Waterloo. Wellington had chosen a defensive position anchored on the farmhouse of Hougoumont and the ridge at Mont St. Jean. His forces were positioned on the high ground. Napoleon launched a series of attacks on the British lines throughout the day, including a massive assault on

Hougoumont. The British, supported by the arrival of Prussian reinforcements under Blücher, held their ground despite heavy casualties. In the late afternoon, Prussian forces arrived in force, threatening Napoleon's right flank. This development forced Napoleon into a desperate last-ditch attack on Wellington's center. The attack on Wellington's center failed, and the French army began to disintegrate. Realizing the battle was lost, Napoleon ordered a retreat.

Napoleon's defeat at Waterloo marked the end of his rule and ambitions. He was exiled to the remote island of Saint Helena in the South Atlantic, where he spent the remainder of his life. The defeat of Napoleon at Waterloo led to the Congress of Vienna, where the European powers sought to redraw the map of Europe and restore order after the upheaval of the Napoleonic Wars. Louis XVIII was restored to the French throne, marking the return of the Bourbon Monarchy.

45. Napoleon's Influence on Modern Europe

Napoleon Bonaparte, one of history's most iconic figures, left an unforgettable mark on Europe that continues to shape the continent's political, social, and cultural landscape to this day. Firstly, it's crucial to acknowledge the undeniable impact of Napoleon's military conquests and reforms on modern Europe. His ambitious campaigns, which extended French control over vast swathes of the continent, not only redrew national boundaries but also introduced a series of reforms that modernized European societies. The Napoleonic Code, for instance, remains a cornerstone of legal systems in several European countries, emphasizing principles of equality before the law, property rights, and secularism. These principles continue to underpin modern legal systems across Europe.

Furthermore, Napoleon's military innovations, including the concept of the citizen army, have had a lasting impact on modern military strategy and tactics. The idea of a conscripted national army became a standard model in Europe and beyond, reshaping the nature of warfare and the relationship between states and their citizens. However, opinions about Napoleon's influence on modern Europe are not solely positive. Critics argue that his militaristic ambitions and expansionist policies led to widespread suffering and loss of life across the continent. The Napoleonic Wars, which spanned over a decade, brought devastation to countless regions and left a legacy of conflict and instability in their wake. Skeptics contend that Napoleon's drive for power disrupted the delicate balance of power in Europe and sowed the seeds for future conflicts, including the two World Wars.

Moreover, Napoleon's impact on national identities in Europe is a subject of debate. While he contributed to the spread of nationalist sentiment in some regions by redrawing boundaries and creating new political entities, he also imposed French cultural norms and institutions on conquered territories. This has led some to argue that his legacy is one of both nation-building and cultural imperialism, with mixed consequences for modern European identities.

In terms of governance, Napoleon's autocratic rule and his establishment of client states have raised questions about the balance between centralized authority and local autonomy. His administrative reforms have been praised for streamlining government functions and modernizing institutions, but they have also been criticized for concentrating power in the hands of the state.

Chapter 10: Stories of Adolf Hitler

Adolf Hitler, a name that still sends shivers down the spine of history, is undeniably one of the most polarizing and consequential figures of the 20th century. Often regarded as the person who altered the course of world history in a way no one could have anticipated, Hitler's impact is both a chilling reminder of the darkest depths humanity can reach and a cautionary tale for generations to come. You can't study European history without coming across Hitler; maybe you've heard "Heil Hitler!" echo through the annals of time, or perhaps the word "Führer" has crossed your path. Hitler's rise to power, marked by his magnetic charisma and ruthlessly efficient political maneuvering, ultimately led to a cataclysmic clash of ideologies that resulted in unimaginable suffering and global conflict.

Adolf Hitler, a name that still sends shivers down the spine of history.[17]

46. The Making of a Dictator: Hitler's Early Years

Adolf Hitler was born on April 20th, 1889, in Braunau am Inn, Austria-Hungary, to Alois Hitler and Klara Pölzl. His childhood was marked by both joys and hardships. Alois Hitler was a stern and occasionally abusive father, while Klara was a gentle and nurturing mother. Young Adolf displayed a talent for drawing but struggled academically. His family moved frequently during his childhood, and he attended several schools in Austria and Germany. This constant upheaval made it challenging for him to form lasting friendships.

From a young age, Hitler showed a talent for drawing, and he harbored dreams of becoming an artist. His early exposure to art came from his mother, Klara, who supported his artistic pursuits and encouraged his creativity. Young Adolf frequently sketched landscapes, buildings, and portraits, often focusing on architectural scenes. In 1907, at the age of 18, Hitler moved to Vienna with the hope of attending the Vienna Academy of Fine Arts, a prestigious institution for aspiring artists. However, his dreams of gaining admission were shattered when he failed the entrance exam. This rejection was a significant blow to his self-esteem and aspirations as an artist.

Life in Vienna during this period was challenging for Hitler. He lived in poverty, eking out a meager existence by selling postcards of his artwork and living in homeless shelters. He often frequented museums and art galleries, where he developed a deep admiration for classical German and Austrian art. It was during his time in Vienna that Hitler began to develop strong nationalistic and anti-Semitic views. He became deeply influenced by the prevalent anti-Semitic rhetoric of the time, and these ideas would later become a central part of his political ideology.

While Hitler continued to produce art throughout his life, his works were met with limited success. His artistic style was primarily focused on landscapes, scenes of architecture, and portraits. His paintings often lacked the innovative and experimental qualities that were gaining popularity in the art world during the early 20th century. Hitler's inability to gain recognition as an artist, combined with his growing disillusionment with life in Vienna, fueled his sense of resentment and bitterness. He began to view himself as a misunderstood genius whose talents had been unfairly ignored.

As World War I erupted in 1914, Hitler saw an opportunity to leave his unfulfilling artistic career behind and enlist as a soldier. His service in the war would prove to be a turning point in his life, leading him down the path of political radicalization and ultimately to the rise of the Nazi Party. In retrospect, Hitler's failure to establish himself as an artist was a crucial factor in his transformation into a dictator. His artistic struggles, combined with his disillusionment with Vienna and his experiences as a soldier in World War I, laid the groundwork for his later political ambitions. The rejection he faced as an artist left him with a deep-seated desire for recognition and power, which he would ultimately seek to fulfill through his political career.

Hitler's experiences as a soldier during World War I would have a profound impact on his worldview. He served as a frontline soldier in the trenches of the Western Front and participated in several significant battles. One of the most notable events occurred during the Battle of the Somme (1916) when he was wounded twice. First, he was injured by a shell blast and later suffered the effects of mustard gas, which temporarily blinded him. During his time in the military, Hitler received the Iron Cross, Second Class, for his bravery and dedication. Despite his wounds, he remained committed to the German cause and saw the war as a noble struggle.

However, it was the outcome of World War I that deeply scarred Hitler. The news of Germany's defeat and the signing of the Armistice in 1918 devastated him. He, like many others, believed that Germany had been betrayed by politicians and blamed Jews, communists, and perceived internal enemies for the nation's downfall.

47. The Beer Hall Putsch: An Attempt at Revolution

As World War I came to an end, Adolf Hitler faced an uncertain future. His dreams of becoming an artist had long since withered in the face of his experiences as a soldier and the harsh realities of post-war Germany. The trauma of the war and his deep resentment towards the Weimar Republic fueled a growing ambition within him. The defeated and demoralized Germany of the early 1920s provided fertile ground for extremist ideologies to take root. Having tasted the intoxicating allure of leadership during his military service, Hitler began to see himself as a savior of Germany, a man with a mission to restore the nation to its former glory.

As he returned to civilian life, he turned his attention toward politics. On the evening of November 8th, 1923, Munich was enveloped in darkness as Adolf Hitler and his band of fervent followers gathered at the Bürgerbräukeller beer hall. Little did the city know that this seemingly ordinary night would witness an audacious coup attempt, known as the Beer Hall Putsch, which would shape the course of history. That evening, Hitler and approximately 2,000 of his loyal supporters organized a rally at the Bürgerbräukeller beer hall to protest the Weimar government and its perceived failings, particularly its handling of the Ruhr Crisis and the economic strife facing the German people.

The atmosphere became increasingly charged with revolutionary fervor as Hitler delivered a fiery speech. He proclaimed the imminent overthrow of the Weimar Republic and the establishment of a "national government." He was joined by prominent figures of the Nazi Party, including Ernst Röhm and Rudolf Hess, both of whom played significant roles in the events that followed. Inspired by Hitler's impassioned speech, the Nazi paramilitary group, the SA (Sturmabteilung), set off on the night of November 8th to seize key government buildings in Munich. Their aim was to force the Bavarian government to join their cause and then march on Berlin to topple the Weimar government.

The Putsch was, however, a hastily planned operation. As the SA members marched through the streets of Munich, they encountered a police blockade at the Feldherrnhalle, a memorial to Bavarian military heroes. A brief but intense firefight ensued. The police quickly overwhelmed the disorganized and ill-equipped SA troops. In the midst of the chaos, Hitler was injured by a stray bullet – dislocating his shoulder. He was subsequently arrested and taken into custody. The Beer Hall Putsch had failed spectacularly as 16 Nazis and four police officers were killed in the skirmish, while many others, including Hitler, were injured. The Weimar government remained firmly in control, and the Nazi Party was banned.

Adolf Hitler and his co-conspirators were put on trial for treason in February 1924. The trial provided Hitler with a high-profile platform to espouse his nationalist and anti-Semitic views, effectively turning the courtroom into a propaganda stage. During the trial, Hitler expressed no remorse for his actions and instead defended his motivations, portraying himself as a patriot. The sympathetic judge handed down a relatively lenient sentence of five years in prison, of which Hitler would serve only nine months. During his incarceration at Landsberg Prison, Hitler penned his infamous autobiography and political manifesto, "Mein Kampf."

While the Beer Hall Putsch appeared to be a failure initially, it had several profound consequences. Firstly, it catapulted Hitler and the Nazi Party into the national spotlight, allowing them to reach a broader audience with their extremist ideology. Secondly, Hitler's trial and imprisonment allowed him to consolidate his ideas, refine his propaganda, and solidify his leadership within the Nazi Party. He emerged from prison with a renewed determination to achieve power through legal means.

48. Hitler's Rise to Power: Exploiting a Nation's Despair

Adolf Hitler's ascent to power in Germany was a testament to his ability to exploit the grievances and fears of a nation reeling from the aftermath of World War I and the economic hardships of the Weimar Republic. Following his release from prison after the failed Beer Hall Putsch in 1923, Hitler embarked on a calculated and strategic path that would lead him to the chancellorship of Germany in 1933. When Hitler was released from prison in December 1924, Germany was grappling with numerous issues that left its citizens disillusioned and discontented. The Treaty of Versailles imposed heavy reparations and territorial losses, leading to economic turmoil, hyperinflation, and widespread unemployment. The Weimar Republic, plagued by political instability and coalition governments, struggled to address these challenges effectively.

After the failure of the Beer Hall Putsch, Hitler realized that a violent coup was not the most viable path to power. He resolved to achieve his goals legally through elections and political maneuvering. Hitler's gift for charismatic and impassioned speeches became a potent weapon. He could tap into the frustrations and fears of the German people, promising them a way out of their suffering. Hitler recognized the power of propaganda in shaping public opinion. He established the Nazi Party's newspaper, "Völkischer Beobachter," and employed Joseph Goebbels to mastermind the dissemination of Nazi propaganda. After the Putsch, the Nazi Party was banned. Hitler worked to rebuild it, drawing in new supporters and expanding its base. The SA, or Brownshirts, served as a paramilitary force that intimidated political opponents.

During the late 1920s and early 1930s, the Nazi Party gained increasing support through a combination of factors. Hitler and the Nazis strategically adapted their message to appeal to a wide range of voters, from nationalists and disaffected veterans to the economically disadvantaged. The frequent collapse of coalition governments, coupled with the inability to address economic problems effectively, disillusioned many Germans with democratic governance. In the July 1930 Reichstag elections, the Nazi Party became the second-largest political party in Germany, securing 18.3% of the vote. This electoral success gave Hitler a prominent position in the political landscape.

In January 1933, following a series of backroom deals and political maneuvering, President Paul von Hindenburg appointed Hitler as Chancellor of Germany. The decision was driven by a belief among conservative politicians that they could control Hitler and that he would provide stability. Hitler's appointment marked the beginning of the end for the Weimar Republic and the erosion of German democracy. He moved quickly to consolidate power, using the Reichstag Fire in February 1933 as a pretext to push through the Reichstag Fire Decree, which suspended civil liberties and allowed for the arrest of political opponents.

Hitler's regime was characterized by its totalitarian control over every aspect of German life. The Nazis suppressed dissent through the brutal secret police, the Gestapo, and silenced opposition through censorship and propaganda. They indoctrinated youth through the Hitler Youth organization and redefined education to align with Nazi ideology. The Nuremberg Laws of 1935 stripped Jews of their rights, segregating them from the rest of society.

One of the most horrifying aspects of Hitler's rule was the Holocaust, a systematic genocide targeting Jews and other minority groups. The Nazis established extermination camps like Auschwitz, Sobibor, and Treblinka, where millions were systematically murdered. The Holocaust resulted in the deaths of six million Jews and millions of others, including Romani people, disabled individuals, and political dissidents. Hitler's fanatical anti-Semitism fueled this unparalleled atrocity. The Holocaust remains a haunting testament to the depths of human cruelty. Entire families were annihilated, and communities were destroyed. The survivors bore lifelong scars, and the trauma of the Holocaust continues to reverberate through generations.

Hitler's expansionist ambitions led to the outbreak of World War II in 1939 when Germany invaded Poland. The war escalated, engulfing Europe and later expanding to other continents. Hitler's military campaigns, including the Blitzkrieg tactics, the invasion of France, and the Eastern Front, resulted in millions of deaths and widespread devastation. The impact of World War II was catastrophic. Cities were reduced to rubble, economies were shattered, and millions of lives were lost. The war's consequences extended far beyond Europe, affecting nations worldwide.

49. Operation Barbarossa: The Turning Point

Operation Barbarossa, launched by Nazi Germany on June 22nd, 1941, marked a pivotal moment in World War II. This massive military campaign, driven by Adolf Hitler's ambitions, saw Germany invade the Soviet Union with the aim of securing Lebensraum (living space) and crippling the Soviet state. While initially successful, the operation ultimately became a turning point in the war due to several key factors. Operation Barbarossa was one of the largest military campaigns in history. It involved three million German soldiers, supported by hundreds of thousands of vehicles and over 3,000 aircraft. The sheer scale and ambition of the invasion demonstrated Hitler's determination to achieve a swift victory over the Soviet Union.

In the early months of the campaign, German forces made significant advances into Soviet territory. They captured vast swaths of land, inflicted heavy casualties on the Red Army, and encircled and captured hundreds of thousands of Soviet soldiers. Key cities like Kyiv and Smolensk fell to the Germans, and the Soviet Union appeared to be on the brink of collapse. However, Operation Barbarossa faced severe logistical challenges. The vast distances of the Soviet Union stretched German supply lines, making it increasingly difficult to sustain the rapid advance. Harsh weather conditions, particularly the brutal Russian winter, exacerbated the logistical woes. German soldiers lacked adequate winter clothing and equipment, leading to frostbite and low morale.

As the German advance slowed due to logistical difficulties and stubborn Soviet resistance, it became evident that the Red Army was far from defeated. The Soviets displayed remarkable resilience and adaptability. They adopted a strategy of scorched-earth tactics, denying the Germans valuable resources as they retreated eastward. The vastness of the Soviet Union allowed for strategic depth, and the Soviets regrouped and launched counteroffensives.

The Battle of Stalingrad, fought from August 23rd, 1942, to February 2nd, 1943, marked a critical turning point in Operation Barbarossa. The city of Stalingrad became a symbol of Soviet resistance, and both sides suffered immense casualties in the brutal street-by-street combat. The Soviets eventually encircled the German Sixth Army, leading to its surrender in February 1943. The loss of the Sixth Army, along with its equipment and personnel, was a devastating blow to the German war effort.

By 1943, Operation Barbarossa had stalled. The Germans faced a protracted war of attrition on the Eastern Front, with neither side able to gain a decisive advantage. Additionally, the Soviet Union's growing strength, aided by lend-lease supplies from the Western Allies, further tilted the balance in favor of the Soviets.

Operation Barbarossa, initially perceived as a campaign of swift victory, had become a quagmire for the Germans. By late 1943 and early 1944, the Soviets had regained much of their lost territory and were advancing into Eastern Europe. The successful

Soviet offensives, including the Battles of Kursk and Bagration, had decisively shifted the momentum of the war. Operation Barbarossa had not achieved its objectives. Instead, it triggered a protracted and costly conflict with the Soviet Union. It marked the beginning of a long retreat for the German army, culminating in the capture of Berlin by Soviet forces in April 1945.

50. The Führer's End: Hitler's Downfall and the Death of Nazism

As the Allies closed in on Germany from both the west and east, the situation on the Eastern Front was particularly dire. The Soviet Red Army, having gained immense strength and momentum, was advancing rapidly. By early 1945, they had entered German territory, capturing key cities like Warsaw and reaching the Oder River, just miles from Berlin. In January 1945, Hitler retreated to his underground bunker in Berlin, known as the Führerbunker. This reinforced complex, located beneath the Reich Chancellery, became the epicenter of Nazi power in the final months of the war. It was here that Hitler and his closest associates, including Eva Braun and Joseph Goebbels, would make their last stand.

Hitler's mental state had deteriorated significantly by this point. He clung to delusional hopes of a miraculous turnaround and continued to issue irrational orders to non-existent armies. He rejected any notion of surrender and vowed to fight to the death. As the Soviet Red Army encircled Berlin in April 1945, the city endured a ferocious and devastating battle. The fighting was characterized by street-to-street combat, heavy artillery bombardments, and widespread destruction. Civilians suffered immensely, and the city's infrastructure crumbled.

In the midst of this chaos, Hitler married Eva Braun on April 29, 1945, in the Führerbunker. The following day, they both committed suicide. Hitler took his own life by swallowing a cyanide capsule and shooting himself in the head, while Eva Braun also ingested poison. Their bodies were later discovered in the bunker. With Berlin under Soviet control and its leaders dead, the remnants of the Nazi regime had no choice but to surrender. On May 7th, 1945, General Alfred Jodl signed the unconditional surrender of all German forces in Reims, France, which came into effect on May 8th, 1945, officially marking the end of World War II in Europe.

The death of Adolf Hitler and the surrender of Nazi Germany brought an end to one of the darkest chapters in history. The horrors of the Holocaust, the devastation wrought by the war, and the scale of human suffering were brought to light as Allied forces liberated concentration camps and occupied German territory. In the aftermath of the war, the leaders of Nazi Germany, including those who had survived and been captured, were brought to justice at the Nuremberg Trials. These trials, held from November 20th, 1945, to October 1st, 1946, prosecuted individuals responsible for war crimes, crimes against humanity, and other atrocities committed during the war.

Conclusion

As you turn the last page of this book, take a moment to appreciate the significance of the narratives you've read about and their lasting impact on the present day. This exploration reminds you of the diverse history that has shaped the continent and continues to influence Europe and the wider world. You've learned all about the epochs of Europe's past, from the awe-inspiring civilizations of Greece and Rome, with their monumental contributions to philosophy, art, and governance, to the tumultuous waves of the Middle Ages, where knights, kings, and peasants each played their part in forging the continent's destiny. You can only marvel at the explosion of creativity during the Renaissance and witnessed the profound transformations brought about by the Enlightenment, an era that championed reason, liberty, and equality.

Throughout these stories, you've also come across individuals whose actions and ideas have reverberated through the ages. From the revolutionary thoughts of Voltaire and Rousseau to the courage of the human rights rebellions, these individuals have left a mark on the course of European history that cannot be erased. However, this learning isn't solely supposed to be an exploration of the past; it serves as a bridge to understanding the present and the future. Europe's history is a living testament to the enduring consequences of past actions. The echoes of empire-building, the lessons learned from devastating wars, and the struggles for democracy and human rights all continue to shape the continent's societies and institutions.

In today's Europe, the product of centuries of interactions, conflicts, and collaborations can be witnessed. The European Union, an entity born from the ashes of World War II, symbolizes Europe's commitment to unity and cooperation, driven by the imperative to prevent another catastrophic conflict. Understanding these stories in their contemporary context is essential. Europe's history is not a distant relic but an ever-present force shaping today's societies, politics, and collective memory. In this increasingly interconnected world, where actions in one part of the globe can have far-reaching consequences, the lessons of history are more vital than ever.

European history isn't just a collection of stories; it's a living legacy that continues to shape the world today. These narratives should inspire you to learn from the past, foster empathy and understanding, and work towards a future that values diversity, champions peace, and upholds the ideals of justice and progress.

Check out another book in the series

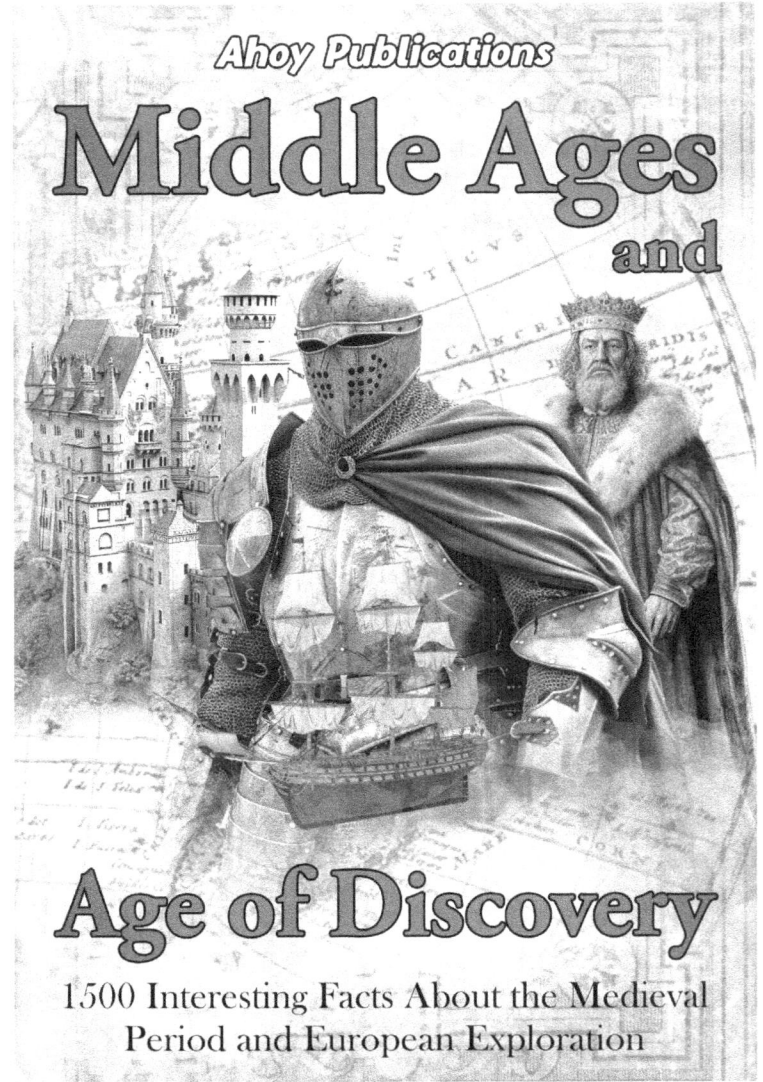

Welcome Aboard, Check Out This Limited-Time Free Bonus!

Ahoy, reader! Welcome to the Ahoy Publications family, and thanks for snagging a copy of this book! Since you've chosen to join us on this journey, we'd like to offer you something special.

Check out the link below for a FREE e-book filled with delightful facts about American History.

But that's not all - you'll also have access to our exclusive email list with even more free e-books and insider knowledge. Well, what are ye waiting for? Click the link below to join and set sail toward exciting adventures in American History.

Access your bonus here: https://ahoypublications.com/

Or, Scan the QR code!

Sources and Additional References

Part 1

"Upper Paleolithic Period." Britannica, Encyclopedia Britannica, Sept. 2020, www.britannica.com/topic/Upper-Paleolithic-period.

"Neolithic Revolution." Encyclopedia Britannica, July 2020, http://www.britannica.com/event/Neolithic-Revolution.

Hingley, Richard. The Bronze Age: A Social and Economic History. Routledge, 2012.

Cunliffe, Barry. The Ancient Celts. Oxford University Press, 1997.

Cunliffe, Barry W., and Chris Gosden. The Oxford Illustrated History of Prehistoric Europe. Oxford University Press, 2001.

Wright, Rachel. "Minoan and Mycenaean Art." Khan Academy, Khan Academy, www.khanacademy.org/humanities/ancient-art-civilizations/aegean/minoan-mycenaean/a/minoan-and-mycenaean-art.

Rosen, Marc. The Iron Age: An Overview. Facts on File, 2006.

Roberts, J.M. History of the World. Oxford University Press, 1993.

"Roman Republic." Encyclopedia Britannica, Mar. 2018, www.britannica.com/topic/Roman-Republic.

"Greco-Persian Wars." Encyclopedia Britannica, Sept. 2018, https://www.britannica.com/event/Greco-Persian-Wars.

Boak, Arthur E. R. A History of Rome to 565 A.D. Macmillan, 1923.

"Migration Period." Ancient History Encyclopedia, Ancient History Encyclopedia, Aug. 2018, www.ancient.eu/migration_period/.

"The Byzantine Empire." History.com. A&E Television Networks, Apr. 2021.

"The Early Middle Ages." Encyclopedia Britannica, May 2017, www.britannica.com/event/Early-Middle-Ages.

Jensen, Jens Christian. "Vikings." Encyclopedia Britannica, May 2019, www.britannica.com/topic/Viking.

"Vikings." History.com, A&E Television Networks, https://www.history.com/topics/vikings

"Charlemagne." Encyclopedia Britannica, Mar. 2020, https://www.britannica.com/biography/Charlemagne.

Hunt, E.D., and Mary Rivier. Medieval Europe: A Short History. McGraw-Hill Education, 2014.

"Art in the Renaissance." Khan Academy. April 15, 2021.
https://www.khanacademy.org/humanities/renaissance-reformation/renaissance-europe/a/renaissance-art.

Kort, Michael. The Age of Exploration: Discovering the New World. Rosen, 2013.

"The Scientific Revolution," Encyclopedia Britannica
https://www.britannica.com/event/Scientific-Revolution

"The Thirty Years' War." History.com, A&E Television Networks, Aug. 2017,
www.history.com/topics/thirty-years-war.

McPhee, Peter. The French Revolution. Routledge, 2017.

"Napoleon Bonaparte." Encyclopedia Britannica, Mar. 2021,
www.britannica.com/biography/Napoleon-Bonaparte

Smith, David. "Industrial Revolution." Encyclopedia Britannica, Feb. 2020,
www.britannica.com/event/Industrial-Revolution.

"Industrial Revolution." History.com, A&E Television Networks, 2009,
www.history.com/topics/industrial-revolution.

"Napoleonic Wars." Encyclopedia Britannica, 2020, https://www.britannica.com/
event/Napoleonic-Wars.

"Greek War of Independence." Encyclopedia Britannica, Oct. 2018,
www.britannica.com/event/Greek-War-of-Independence.

"The Crimean War." History, A&E Television Networks, 2020,
www.history.com/topics/crimean-war.

"German Unification." History.com, A&E Television Networks, 2021,
www.history.com/topics/german-unification.

"1848 Revolutions." Encyclopedia Britannica, Feb. 2021,
https://www.britannica.com/event/1848-Revolutions.

"Scramble for Africa." History.com, A&E Television Networks,
https://www.history.com/topics/africa/scramble-for-africa.

"World War I." History.com, A&E Television Networks, www.history.com/topics/world-war-i/world-war-i-history.

"WWI Casualties and Statistics." History Learning Site,
www.historylearningsite.co.uk/world-war-one/world-war-one-casualties-statistics/.

"Soviet Union." Encyclopedia Britannica, June 2021, www.britannica.com/place/ Soviet-Union.

"A Brief History of the Russian Revolution." History.com, A&E Television Networks, Aug. 2016, www.history.com/topics/russia/russian-revolution.

"World War II." History.com, A&E Television Networks,
https://www.history.com/topics/world-war-ii.

"The Holocaust." United States Holocaust Memorial Museum,
https://www.ushmm.org/learn/timeline-of-events/the-holocaust.

"The Cold War." History, A&E Television Networks, www.history.com/topics/cold-war.

"WWII and Decolonization." The History Channel, A&E Television Networks, LLC, https://www.history.com/topics/world-war-ii/wwii-and-decolonization.

"History of the European Union." Europa, European Commission, https://europa.eu/european-union/about-eu/history_en.

"The Prague Spring'." Britannica, The Editors of Encyclopedia Britannica, www.britannica.com/event/Prague-Spring.

"Yugoslav Wars." Britannica, The Editors of Encyclopedia Britannica, Jan. 2020, www.britannica.com/event/Yugoslav-wars.

Part 2

(n.d.). Wordpress.Com. https://mrcaseyhistory.files.wordpress.com/2019/02/vikings-raiders-or-traders.pdf

(N.d.-a). Uchicago.edu. https://penelope.uchicago.edu/~grout/encyclopaedia_romana/miscellanea/cleopatra/egypt.html#:~:text=Julius%20Caesar%20defeated%20Ptolemy%20XII,XIII%20on%20the%20Egyptian%20throne.

(N.d.-b). Historyofinformation.com. https://www.historyofinformation.com/detail.php?entryid=3337

1769-1793: Napoleon Bonaparte's early years. (n.d.). Napoleon.org. https://www.napoleon.org/en/history-of-the-two-empires/timelines/1769-1793-napoleon-bonapartes-early-years/

Adolf Hitler: Rise to power, impact & death. (2009, October 29). HISTORY. https://www.history.com/topics/world-war-ii/adolf-hitler-1

Anastasi, L. (2023, April 23). The Siege of Paris: City Under Fire. Medieval History – Yesterday in a Nutshell. https://historymedieval.com/the-siege-of-paris-city-under-fire/

Ancient Greek Democracy. (2018, August 23). HISTORY. https://www.history.com/topics/ancient-greece/ancient-greece-democracy

Beer hall putsch. (2009, November 9). HISTORY. https://www.history.com/topics/european-history/beer-hall-putsch

Bertocchi, G. (2016). The legacies of slavery in and out of Africa. IZA Journal of Migration, 5(1). https://doi.org/10.1186/s40176-016-0072-0

Beware the Ides of March: Julius Caesar's assassination in art. (n.d.). Artuk.org. https://artuk.org/discover/stories/beware-the-ides-of-march-julius-caesars-assassination-in-art

Birth of the Vikings. (n.d.). Sky HISTORY TV Channel. https://www.history.co.uk/shows/vikings/articles/birth-of-the-vikings

Black Death – Bubonic Plague, Europe, 1347. (n.d.). In Encyclopedia Britannica.

British Library. (n.d.). Www.Bl.UK ; The British Library.

British Library. (n.d.). Www.Bl.UK ; The British Library

Caesar crosses the Rubicon. (n.d.). Nationalgeographic.org. https://education.nationalgeographic.org/resource/caesar-crosses-rubicon/

Campbell, E. M. J., & Fernandez-Armesto, F. (2023). Vasco da Gama. In Encyclopedia Britannica.

Cartwright, M. (2016). Pizarro & the Fall of the Inca Empire. World History Encyclopedia. https://www.worldhistory.org/article/915/pizarro--the-fall-of-the-inca-empire/

Cartwright, M. (2020). Peasants' Revolt. World History Encyclopedia.

Cartwright, M. (2021). Vasco da Gama. World History Encyclopedia. https://www.worldhistory.org/Vasco_da_Gama/

Cartwright, M. (2023). Athenian Democracy. World History Encyclopedia. https://www.worldhistory.org/Athenian_Democracy/

Cartwright, M. (2023). Black Death. World History Encyclopedia. https://www.worldhistory.org/Black_Death/

Chintaluri, A., & Chintaluri, A. (2022, April 18). The Ancient Agora of Athens – Everything you Need to Know to Plan a Visit [Video]. Headout Blog. https://www.headout.com/blog/agora-of-athens/

Christopher Columbus Reaches the "New World." (2009, November 24). HISTORY. https://www.history.com/this-day-in-history/columbus-reaches-the-new-world

Christopher Columbus. (2009, November 9). HISTORY. https://www.history.com/topics/exploration/christopher-columbus

Columbus Lands in South America. (2010, July 21). HISTORY. https://www.history.com/this-day-in-history/columbus-lands-in-south-america

Constitutional Rights Foundation. (n.d.). Crf-usa.org. https://www.crf-usa.org/bill-of-rights-in-action/bria-26-2-the-black-death-a-catastrophe-in-medieval-europe.html

Decameron web. (n.d.-a). Brown.edu. https://www.brown.edu/Departments/Italian_Studies/dweb/plague/effects/social.php

Decameron web. (n.d.-b). Brown.edu. https://www.brown.edu/Departments/Italian_Studies/dweb/plague/effects/social.php

Dow, D. (n.d.). Who killed Julius Caesar & why was he betrayed? Magellantv.com. https://www.magellantv.com/articles/who-killed-julius-caesar-why-was-he-betrayed

French revolutionaries storm the Bastille. (2009, November 24). HISTORY. https://www.history.com/this-day-in-history/french-revolutionaries-storm-bastille

Garcia, B. (2018). Romulus and Remus. World History Encyclopedia. https://www.worldhistory.org/Romulus_and_Remus/

Gill, N. (2018). Ecclesia, the Greek Assembly. ThoughtCo. https://www.thoughtco.com/ecclesia-assembly-of-athens-118833

Greece; The Pros and Cons of Democracy Therein – 2680 Words | Bartleby. (n.d.). https://www.bartleby.com/essay/Greece-The-Pros-and-Cons-of-Democracy-P3MAPS83DRVA

Greek City-States. (n.d.). https://education.nationalgeographic.org/resource/greek-city-states/

Greenspan, J. (2012, June 22). Why was Napoleon's invasion of Russia the beginning of the end? HISTORY. https://www.history.com/news/napoleons-disastrous-invasion-of-russia

History & Policy. (n.d.). History & Policy. https://www.historyandpolicy.org/policy-papers/papers/the-economic-consequences-of-plague-lessons-for-the-age-of-covid-19

Holmes, R. C. L. (2021, January 16). The Gallic Wars: How Julius Caesar conquered Gaul (modern France). TheCollector. https://www.thecollector.com/gallic-wars-how-julius-caesar-conquered-gaul/

How did Julius Caesar rise to power? (n.d.). Ipl.org. https://www.ipl.org/essay/How-Did-Julius-Caesar-Rise-To-Power-PC9XYVHT8SM

Hudson, M. (2023). Battle of Tenochtitlán. In Encyclopedia Britannica.

Introduction to Kant's "What Is Enlightenment?" (n.d.). K-State.Edu. https://www.k-state.edu/english/baker/english233/Kant-WIE-intro.htm

Jarus, O. (2020, March 11). Lindisfarne: The "Holy Island" where Vikings spilled the "blood of saints." Livescience.Com; Live Science. https://www.livescience.com/lindisfarne.html

Johnson, N., Koyama, M., & Jedwab, R. (n.d.). Pandemics, places, and populations: Evidence from the Black Death. CEPR. https://cepr.org/voxeu/columns/pandemics-places-and-populations-evidence-black-death

Julius Caesar Crosses the Rubicon, 49 BC. (n.d.). Eyewitnesstohistory.com. http://www.eyewitnesstohistory.com/caesar.htm

How the First Triumvirate changed ancient Rome. (n.d.). History Skills. https://www.historyskills.com/classroom/ancient-history/anc-1st-triumvirate-reading/

Wasson, D. L. (2016). First Triumvirate. World History Encyclopedia. https://www.worldhistory.org/First_Triumvirate/

Julius Caesar. (n.d.). Nationalgeographic.org. https://education.nationalgeographic.org/resource/julius-caesar/

Julius Caesar's rise to power and dictatorship. (2022, September 15). Edubirdie. https://edubirdie.com/examples/julius-caesars-rise-to-power-and-dictatorship/

Lesso, R. (2022). What Were the City States of Ancient Greece? TheCollector. https://www.thecollector.com/what-were-the-city-states-of-ancient-greece/

Life and Teachings of Jesus. (n.d.). Pluralism.Org. https://pluralism.org/life-and-teachings-of-jesus

Little, B. (2023, July 13). Cleopatra's complicated inner circle: Siblings, successors, and lovers. HISTORY. https://www.history.com/news/cleopatras-complicated-inner-circle-siblings-successors-and-lovers

Lochun, K. (2020, December 21). Who were the Kievan Rus, and what do they have to do with the Vikings? HistoryExtra. https://www.historyextra.com/period/viking/rus-vikings-kievan-rus-rurik-vladimir-great/

Marco, S. (2023, March 14). Caesar and Cleopatra in Egypt. Odysseytraveller.com; Odyssey Traveller. https://www.odysseytraveller.com/articles/caesar-and-cleopatra-in-egypt/

Mark, H. W. (2023). Battle of Austerlitz. World History Encyclopedia. https://www.worldhistory.org/article/2253/battle-of-austerlitz/

Mark, J. J. (2018). Kievan Rus. World History Encyclopedia. https://www.worldhistory.org/Kievan_Rus/

Mark, J. J. (2020). Effects of the Black Death on Europe. World History Encyclopedia. https://www.worldhistory.org/article/1543/effects-of-the-black-death-on-europe/

Martinez, J. (2023). The Medici Family: Ultimate Power and Legacy In The Renaissance. TheCollector. https://www.thecollector.com/the-medici-family-legacy/

McLean, J. (n.d.-a). Napoleon's defeat at Waterloo. Lumenlearning.com. https://courses.lumenlearning.com/suny-hccc-worldhistory2/chapter/napoleons-defeat-at-waterloo/

McLean, J. (n.d.-b). The Napoleonic code. Lumenlearning.com. https://courses.lumenlearning.com/suny-hccc-worldhistory2/chapter/the-napoleonic-code/

Medievalists.net. (2023, July 18). How Christianity came to Medieval Europe. Medievalists.Net. https://www.medievalists.net/2023/07/christianity-medieval-europe/

Moya, M. J. (2022, March 17). Saint Patrick, the man behind the St. Patrick's Day holiday, wasn't even Irish. USA Today. https://www.usatoday.com/story/news/2022/03/17/st-patrick-day-saint/7039195001/

Napoleon Bonaparte. (2009, November 9). HISTORY. https://www.history.com/topics/european-history/napoleon

Napoleon Bonaparte. (2020, October 11). BYJUS; BYJU'S. https://byjus.com/free-ias-prep/napoleon-bonaparte/

Napoleon invades Russia. (n.d.). Nationalgeographic.org. https://education.nationalgeographic.org/resource/napoleon-invades-russia/

Napoleonic Code approved in France. (2010, February 9). HISTORY. https://www.history.com/this-day-in-history/napoleonic-code-approved-in-france

ODYSSEY/Rome. (n.d.). Emory.edu. https://carlos.emory.edu/htdocs/ODYSSEY/ROME/romulus.html

Operation Barbarossa: why Hitler's invasion of the Soviet Union was his greatest mistake. (2021, March 3). HistoryExtra. https://www.historyextra.com/period/second-world-war/operation-barbarossa-hitlers-greatest-mistake/

Pagan to Christian: The Transformation of Rome. (2017, April 17). Brewminate: A Bold Blend of News and Ideas. https://brewminate.com/pagan-to-christian-the-transformation-of-rome/

Pandemics and the persecution of minorities: Evidence from the Black Death. (n.d.). CEPR. https://cepr.org/voxeu/columns/pandemics-and-persecution-minorities-evidence-black-death

PBS — Napoleon: Napoleon at war. (n.d.). Pbs.org. https://www.pbs.org/empires/napoleon/n_war/campaign/page_6.html

Persecution of the Jews — insects, disease, and history. (n.d.). Montana.edu. https://www.montana.edu/historybug/yersiniaessays/pariera-dinkins.html

Pirie, M. (2019, May 30). Voltaire, champion of freedom —. Adam Smith Institute. https://www.adamsmith.org/blog/voltaire-champion-of-freedom

Rattini, K. B. (2019, February 20). Julius Caesar—facts and information. National Geographic. https://www.nationalgeographic.com/culture/article/julius-caesar

Renaissance Period: Timeline, Art & Facts. (2018, April 4). HISTORY. https://www.history.com/topics/renaissance/renaissance

Ritzmann, I. (1998). The Black Death as a cause of the massacres of Jews: a myth of medical history? Medizin, Gesellschaft, Und Geschichte: Jahrbuch Des Instituts Für Geschichte Der Medizin Der Robert Bosch Stiftung, 17. https://pubmed.ncbi.nlm.nih.gov/11625662/

Roosen, J., & Curtis, D. R. (2019). The 'light touch' of the Black Death in the Southern Netherlands: an urban trick: THE BLACK DEATH IN THE SOUTHERN NETHERLANDS. The Economic History Review, 72(1), 32–56. https://doi.org/10.1111/ehr.12667

Russell, E., University of Cambridge, Parker, M., & University of Bristol. (2020, July 2). How the Black Death made the rich richer. BBC. https://www.bbc.com/worklife/article/20200701-how-the-black-death-make-the-rich-richer

Sakoulas, T. (n.d.). The Agora of Athens. This Page and All Its Contents Are Copyright © 2002-today, Ancient-Greece.org. All Rights Reserved. For Copyright Release Information, See the About Page. https://www.ancient-greece.org/archaeology/agora.html

Singh, A. (2021, February 19). The early life of Adolf Hitler. Wondrium Daily.

Singh, A. (2022, April 25). Black Death and Medieval People: Resilience during a Pandemic. Wondrium Daily

Taylor, A. (2011, October 16). World War II: The Holocaust. Atlantic Monthly (Boston, Mass.: 1993). https://www.theatlantic.com/photo/2011/10/world-war-ii-the-holocaust/100170/

The economic impact of the black death. (n.d.). .eh.net. https://eh.net/encyclopedia/the-economic-impact-of-the-black-death/

The Editors of Encyclopaedia Britannica. (1998, July 20). Sforza Family | Italian Renaissance, Milan & Politics. Encyclopedia Britannica. https://www.britannica.com/topic/family-kinship

The Editors of Encyclopaedia Britannica. (2023, March 10). Council of Five Hundred | Athens, Ancient Greece, & Definition. Encyclopedia Britannica. https://www.britannica.com/topic/Council-of-Five-Hundred-ancient-Greek-council

The Editors of Encyclopedia Britannica. (2011). Roman republican calendar. In Encyclopedia Britannica.

The Editors of Encyclopedia Britannica. (2023). Treaty of Tordesillas. In Encyclopedia Britannica.

The Great Courses. (2017, December 1). Caesar's road to the Rubicon—Rome goes to war. Wondrium Daily.

The Great Courses. (2017, October 12). Who was Napoleon Bonaparte? The Early Years. Wondrium Daily.

The Julian calendar takes effect for the first time on New Year's Day. (2010, July 21). HISTORY. https://www.history.com/this-day-in-history/new-years-day

The Munich Putsch – The Holocaust Explained: Designed for schools. (n.d.). Theholocaustexplained.org. https://www.theholocaustexplained.org/the-nazi-rise-to-power/the-early-years-of-the-nazi-party/the-beer-hall-putsch/

The Peasants' Revolt. (2022, February 25). BBC. https://www.bbc.co.uk/bitesize/topics/z93txbk/articles/zyb77yc

The Rise of napoleon. (n.d.). Studentsofhistory.com. https://www.studentsofhistory.com/the-rise-of-napoleon

The Roman Empire: A brief history. (n.d.). Mpm.edu. https://www.mpm.edu/research-collections/anthropology/anthropology-collections-research/mediterranean-oil-lamps/roman-empire-brief-history

The Roman Empire: In the first century. The Roman Empire. Emperors. Julius Caeser. (n.d.). Pbs.org. https://www.pbs.org/empires/romans/empire/julius_caesar.html

The Romans – Roman government. (2013, November 19). History. https://www.historyonthenet.com/the-romans-roman-government

The Sforza Family. (n.d.). https://www.sgira.org/patrons_sforza.htm

The trans-Atlantic slave trade · African passages, lowcountry adaptations lowcountry digital history initiative. (n.d.). Cofc.edu.

https://ldhi.library.cofc.edu/exhibits/show/africanpassageslowcountryadapt/introducti onatlanticworld/trans_atlantic_slave_trade

Treaty of Tordesillas. (n.d.). Nationalgeographic.org. https://education.nationalgeographic.org/resource/treaty-tordesillas/

Vernon, J. (2023, March 14). The Ides of March—a day of murder that forever changed history. National Geographic. https://www.nationalgeographic.com/history/article/julius-caesar-ides-of-march

Volle, A. (2023). storming of the Bastille. In Encyclopedia Britannica.

Wareing, J. (2018, November 30). How Rome came to be ruled by emperors. Highbrow. https://gohighbrow.com/how-rome-came-to-be-ruled-by-emperors/

Watts, E. (2020, October 27). Pagan complacency and the birth of the Christian Roman empire. Aeon; Aeon Magazine. https://aeon.co/essays/pagan-complacency-and-the-birth-of-the-christian-roman-empire

What was Operation "Barbarossa"? (n.d.). Imperial War Museums. https://www.iwm.org.uk/history/what-was-operation-barbarossa

When the Vikings ruled in Britain: A brief history of Danelaw. (n.d.). Sky HISTORY TV Channel. https://www.history.co.uk/articles/when-the-vikings-ruled-in-britain-a-brief-history-of-danelaw

Wilde, R. (2019). The Rise and Fall of the Borgia Family. ThoughtCo. https://www.thoughtco.com/the-borgias-infamous-family-of-renaissance-italy-1221656

World war II and the holocaust, 1939–1945 — United States holocaust memorial museum. (n.d.). Ushmm.org. https://www.ushmm.org/learn/holocaust/path-to-nazi-genocide/chapter-4/world-war-ii-and-the-holocaust-1939-1945

Xviii, L. (2009, November 6). Battle of Waterloo. HISTORY. https://www.history.com/topics/european-history/battle-of-waterloo

Zarevich, E. R. (2021, July 1). How the Black Death led to the Peasants' Revolt. Explorethearchive.com; Open Road Media. https://explorethearchive.com/peasants-revolt

Image Sources

[1] *Γ. Ψάλτης, Public domain, via Wikimedia Commons.*
https://commons.wikimedia.org/wiki/File:Map_of_Athens,_1890.jpg

[2] *http://www.ohiochannel.org/, Attribution, via Wikimedia Commons:*
https://commons.wikimedia.org/wiki/File:Cleisthenes.jpg

[3] *Walter Pompe, CC BY-SA 4.0 <https://creativecommons.org/licenses/by-sa/4.0>, via Wikimedia Commons:*
https://commons.wikimedia.org/wiki/File:Walter_Pompe,_De_Romeinse_wolvin_met_Romulus_en_Remus-_La_louve_romaine_avec_Romulus_et_Remus,_KBS-FRB.jpg

[4] *https://commons.wikimedia.org/wiki/File:Cleopatra_and_Caesar_by_Jean-Leon-Gerome.jpg*

[5] *Pasquale Paolo Cardo from Finale Ligure (Savona), Italy, CC BY 2.0 <https://creativecommons.org/licenses/by/2.0>, via Wikimedia Commons. https://commons.wikimedia.org/wiki/File:Circello_-_The_Little_Baby_Jesus_(24169449556).jpg*

[6] *Nheyob, CC BY-SA 4.0 <https://creativecommons.org/licenses/by-sa/4.0>, via Wikimedia Commons:*
https://commons.wikimedia.org/wiki/File:Saint_Patrick_Catholic_Church_(Junction_City,_Ohio)_-_stained_glass,_Saint_Patrick_-_detail.jpg

[7] *U+1F360, CC BY-SA 4.0 <https://creativecommons.org/licenses/by-sa/4.0>, via Wikimedia Commons.*
https://commons.wikimedia.org/wiki/File:Vikings_Undead.jpg

[8] *Hel-hama, CC BY-SA 3.0 <https://creativecommons.org/licenses/by-sa/3.0>, via Wikimedia Commons:*
https://commons.wikimedia.org/wiki/File:England_878.svg

[9] *https://commons.wikimedia.org/wiki/File:Doutielt3.jpg*

[10] *https://commons.wikimedia.org/wiki/File:Last_Judgement_by_Michelangelo.jpg*

[11] *https://commons.wikimedia.org/wiki/File:Cesareborgia.jpg*

[12] *https://commons.wikimedia.org/wiki/File:The_first_sight_of_the_new_world_-_Columbus_discovering_America_LCCN2006678625.tif*

[13] *https://commons.wikimedia.org/wiki/File:Greg%C3%B3rio_Lopes_-_Vasco_da_Gama_(ca_1524).jpg*

[14] *Snow Minister, CC BY-SA 4.0 <https://creativecommons.org/licenses/by-sa/4.0>, via Wikimedia Commons.*
https://commons.wikimedia.org/wiki/File:Enlightenment_.png

[15] *https://commons.wikimedia.org/wiki/File:Immanuel_Kant_3.jpg*

[16] *https://commons.wikimedia.org/wiki/File:Napoleon_I_of_France_by_Andrea_Appiani.jpg*

[17] *Sashi Suseshi, CC BY-SA 4.0 <https://creativecommons.org/licenses/by-sa/4.0>, via Wikimedia Commons.*
https://commons.wikimedia.org/wiki/File:Adolf_Hitler_in_Color.jpg